# AI AND AUTOMATION WITH PYTHON

## Simplifying Complex Tasks with Python for AI and Automation

## THOMPSON CARTER

# TABLE OF CONTENTS

**INTRODUCTION** .......................................................................... **11**

WHAT YOU WILL LEARN IN THIS BOOK: .....................................12

WHY PYTHON FOR AUTOMATION? .............................................13

WHO THIS BOOK IS FOR: ...........................................................14

HOW TO USE THIS BOOK: ...........................................................15

**CHAPTER 1: INTRODUCTION TO AI AND AUTOMATION
WITH PYTHON** .......................................................................... **18**

UNDERSTANDING AI AND AUTOMATION......................................18

HOW PYTHON FACILITATES AI TASKS.........................................20

REAL-WORLD EXAMPLES OF AI-DRIVEN AUTOMATION...........22

**CHAPTER 2: SETTING UP YOUR PYTHON ENVIRONMENT
FOR AI AND AUTOMATION** .....................................................**27**

INSTALLING NECESSARY LIBRARIES AND TOOLS.........................27

SETTING UP PYTHON, JUPYTER, AND VIRTUAL ENVIRONMENTS ............31

EXAMPLE: A SIMPLE PYTHON SCRIPT FOR AUTOMATION...........33

**CHAPTER 3: THE BASICS OF PYTHON FOR AUTOMATION 37**

CORE PYTHON CONCEPTS FOR AUTOMATION .............................37

FUNCTIONS, LOOPS, AND CONDITIONALS IN AUTOMATION TASKS .........39

EXAMPLE: AUTOMATING A FILE RENAMING TASK.................................42

## CHAPTER 4: PYTHON LIBRARIES FOR AI AND AUTOMATION.................................................................................46

INTRODUCTION TO POPULAR LIBRARIES: NUMPY, PANDAS, SCIKIT-LEARN.................................................................................................46

LIBRARIES FOR WEB SCRAPING, TASK SCHEDULING, AND AUTOMATION
.................................................................................................................50

## CHAPTER 5: INTRODUCTION TO MACHINE LEARNING FOR AUTOMATION.........................................................................56

UNDERSTANDING MACHINE LEARNING BASICS...........................................56

SUPERVISED VS. UNSUPERVISED LEARNING................................................58

EXAMPLE: AUTOMATING PREDICTIONS WITH MACHINE LEARNING MODELS.................................................................................................60

## CHAPTER 6: DATA PREPROCESSING FOR AI...........................66

TECHNIQUES FOR CLEANING AND PREPARING DATA..................................66

HANDLING MISSING VALUES......................................................................67

SCALING DATA.........................................................................................69

ENCODING CATEGORICAL VARIABLES........................................................71

EXAMPLE: PREPROCESSING REAL-WORLD SALES DATA FOR AUTOMATION............................................................................................73

## CHAPTER 7: WORKING WITH APIS FOR AUTOMATION.......76

INTRODUCTION TO APIS AND HOW TO USE THEM WITH PYTHON............76

AUTHENTICATION AND DATA REQUESTS........................................77

EXAMPLE: AUTOMATING DATA RETRIEVAL FROM A WEATHER API......79

**CHAPTER 8: WEB SCRAPING FOR AUTOMATION ..................85**

USING PYTHON FOR WEB SCRAPING AND AUTOMATING DATA
EXTRACTION.................................................................................85

TOOLS FOR WEB SCRAPING .........................................................86

EXAMPLE: AUTOMATING THE EXTRACTION OF PRODUCT PRICES FROM
AN E-COMMERCE SITE ..................................................................90

**CHAPTER 9: TASK SCHEDULING AND AUTOMATION WITH
PYTHON ......................................................................................94**

AUTOMATING RECURRING TASKS WITH SCHEDULERS LIKE CRON OR
TASK SCHEDULER .........................................................................94

USING CRON FOR TASK SCHEDULING (LINUX/MACOS) .................95

USING TASK SCHEDULER FOR TASK SCHEDULING (WINDOWS)...............97

SCHEDULING SCRIPTS TO RUN AT SPECIFIC TIMES ........................98

EXAMPLE: AUTOMATING DAILY EMAIL REPORTS ..........................99

**CHAPTER 10: INTRODUCTION TO NATURAL LANGUAGE
PROCESSING (NLP)...................................................................103**

BASIC NLP CONCEPTS AND PYTHON LIBRARIES (SPACY, NLTK)........ 103

PREPROCESSING AND TOKENIZATION ......................................... 105

EXAMPLE: AUTOMATING TEXT ANALYSIS FOR CUSTOMER FEEDBACK
................................................................................................ 108

**CHAPTER 11: BUILDING SIMPLE AI MODELS WITH PYTHON**
**................................................................................................ 112**

INTRODUCTION TO BUILDING AI MODELS USING SCIKIT-LEARN.......... 112
REGRESSION, CLASSIFICATION, AND CLUSTERING .................................... 113
EXAMPLE: PREDICTING CUSTOMER CHURN WITH PYTHON .................... 115

**CHAPTER 12: AUTOMATING MACHINE LEARNING**
**WORKFLOWS ................................................................................ 121**

END-TO-END AUTOMATION OF ML WORKFLOWS .................................... 121
USING LIBRARIES LIKE MLFLOW AND TENSORFLOW ............................. 122
EXAMPLE: AUTOMATING THE TRAINING AND TESTING OF A MODEL .. 124

**CHAPTER 13: INTRODUCTION TO DEEP LEARNING FOR**
**AUTOMATION ............................................................................... 130**

UNDERSTANDING NEURAL NETWORKS AND DEEP LEARNING.............. 130
LIBRARIES FOR DEEP LEARNING: TENSORFLOW AND KERAS ................ 132
EXAMPLE: AUTOMATING IMAGE RECOGNITION TASKS WITH DEEP
LEARNING ................................................................................................ 134

**CHAPTER 14: COMPUTER VISION FOR AUTOMATION ....... 139**

USING PYTHON FOR IMAGE PROCESSING AND AUTOMATION ............... 139

LIBRARIES FOR COMPUTER VISION IN PYTHON ........................................ 139

IMAGE PROCESSING FOR AUTOMATION ..................................................... 141

EXAMPLE: AUTOMATING OBJECT DETECTION IN VIDEO FEEDS ........... 143

## CHAPTER 15: VOICE RECOGNITION AND AUTOMATION WITH PYTHON ......................................................................... 148

INTEGRATING SPEECH RECOGNITION INTO AUTOMATION TASKS ......... 148

LIBRARIES FOR SPEECH RECOGNITION IN PYTHON ................................ 148

EXAMPLE: AUTOMATING VOICE COMMANDS FOR SMART HOME DEVICES .................................................................................................... 150

EXTENDING THE AUTOMATION SYSTEM ................................................... 154

## CHAPTER 16: BUILDING CHATBOTS WITH PYTHON FOR AUTOMATION ................................................................................ 156

INTRODUCTION TO CHATBOTS AND THEIR USES .................................... 156

USING FRAMEWORKS LIKE CHATTERBOT AND RASA ............................ 157

EXAMPLE: AUTOMATING CUSTOMER SERVICE WITH A PYTHON-POWERED CHATBOT .................................................................................. 161

EXTENDING THE CHATBOT FOR MORE ADVANCED FEATURES .............. 164

## CHAPTER 17: AUTOMATING WEB INTERACTION WITH PYTHON ........................................................................................ 166

USING SELENIUM TO AUTOMATE WEB BROWSING TASKS .................... 166

KEY FEATURES OF SELENIUM ................................................................. 167

INSTALLATION OF SELENIUM AND WEBDRIVER .................................... 167

AUTOMATING WEB INTERACTIONS ............................................... 168

EXAMPLE: AUTOMATING LOGIN AND DATA SUBMISSION ON A WEBSITE

....................................................................................................... 172

## CHAPTER 18: AUTOMATING DATA ANALYSIS AND REPORTING WITH PYTHON .................................................... 176

USING PYTHON FOR AUTOMATED DATA ANALYSIS TASKS .................. 176

KEY LIBRARIES FOR DATA ANALYSIS IN PYTHON ................................ 176

AUTOMATING DATA ANALYSIS WITH PYTHON.................................... 179

## CHAPTER 19: AI-POWERED AUTOMATION FOR BUSINESS OPERATIONS........................................................................... 186

IMPLEMENTING AI AND AUTOMATION IN BUSINESS PROCESSES .......... 186

STREAMLINING TASKS LIKE INVENTORY MANAGEMENT AND

SCHEDULING.......................................................................................... 187

EXAMPLE: AUTOMATING ORDER FULFILLMENT USING AI.................... 189

## CHAPTER 20: CLOUD AUTOMATION WITH PYTHON ......... 195

INTRODUCTION TO CLOUD PLATFORMS LIKE AWS, GCP, AND AZURE 195

AUTOMATING CLOUD RESOURCE MANAGEMENT WITH PYTHON SDKS

....................................................................................................... 197

EXAMPLE: AUTOMATING CLOUD STORAGE MANAGEMENT USING

BOTO3 ON AWS ................................................................................... 198

## CHAPTER 21: INTEGRATING PYTHON WITH IOT FOR AUTOMATION ........................................................................204

CONNECTING PYTHON WITH IOT DEVICES FOR AUTOMATION ............. 204

LIBRARIES AND TOOLS FOR IOT INTEGRATION ........................................ 205

EXAMPLE: AUTOMATING SMART HOME TASKS WITH PYTHON ............. 207

## CHAPTER 22: AUTOMATION WITH PYTHON IN DATA ENGINEERING ..........................................................................213

AUTOMATING ETL (EXTRACT, TRANSFORM, LOAD) PROCESSES ......... 213

USING PYTHON FOR DATA PIPELINES AND AUTOMATION ..................... 214

EXAMPLE: BUILDING AN AUTOMATED DATA PIPELINE FOR ANALYSIS ................................................................................................................ 216

## CHAPTER 23: HANDLING ERRORS AND OPTIMIZING PYTHON AUTOMATION SCRIPTS ...........................................222

DEBUGGING AND ERROR HANDLING IN AUTOMATION SCRIPTS ........... 222

IMPROVING EFFICIENCY AND REDUCING BOTTLENECKS ....................... 225

EXAMPLE: OPTIMIZING AN AUTOMATION SCRIPT FOR FASTER PERFORMANCE ................................................................................................. 227

## CHAPTER 24: SECURING PYTHON-BASED AUTOMATION SYSTEMS ....................................................................................232

BEST PRACTICES FOR SECURING AUTOMATION WORKFLOWS ............. 232

HANDLING SENSITIVE DATA, AUTHENTICATION, AND API SECURITY 233

EXAMPLE: IMPLEMENTING OAUTH FOR SECURE API ACCESS IN
AUTOMATION SCRIPTS ................................................................................. 235

## CHAPTER 25: MONITORING AND MAINTAINING AUTOMATED SYSTEMS .............................................................. 241

TOOLS AND TECHNIQUES FOR MONITORING AUTOMATED SYSTEMS ... 241
LOGGING AND ALERTING FOR TASK FAILURES ......................................... 243
EXAMPLE: SETTING UP MONITORING FOR AUTOMATED BACKUPS ...... 246

## CHAPTER 26: FUTURE TRENDS IN AI AND AUTOMATION WITH PYTHON ........................................................................... 251

EXPLORING FUTURE TECHNOLOGIES AND ADVANCEMENTS ................. 251
THE ROLE OF AI AND AUTOMATION IN DIFFERENT INDUSTRIES .......... 254
EXAMPLE: HOW PYTHON WILL CONTINUE TO SHAPE AUTOMATION IN
THE FUTURE ................................................................................................. 257

# Introduction

In today's fast-paced and technology-driven world, automation has become an essential part of every industry, transforming business processes and operations. From healthcare and manufacturing to finance and logistics, automation is streamlining tasks, reducing human error, and improving efficiency. With advancements in Artificial Intelligence (AI) and machine learning, the scope of automation has expanded significantly, enabling businesses to achieve higher productivity and make data-driven decisions in real-time.

**Python** is one of the most widely used programming languages in the world, and its role in automation is undeniable. As an easy-to-learn, versatile, and powerful language, Python has become the go-to choice for building automation systems, especially those powered by AI. Its vast ecosystem of libraries, frameworks, and tools makes Python the perfect language for automating everything from basic administrative tasks to complex AI-driven workflows. Whether you're an individual developer or part of a larger team, Python's simplicity, flexibility, and strong community support allow you to efficiently build and manage automated systems.

This book, **AI and Automation with Python: Simplifying Complex Tasks with Python for AI and Automation**, aims to provide a comprehensive guide to understanding how Python can be utilized for automating a wide range of tasks. Whether you are a beginner looking to learn the basics of automation or an experienced developer seeking to enhance your knowledge of AI-powered automation systems, this book will walk you through the key concepts, tools, and techniques required to build reliable and efficient automation workflows.

## What You Will Learn in This Book:

Throughout this book, we will cover several critical topics, from the foundational concepts of automation to advanced topics such as integrating Python with AI technologies and IoT systems. Each chapter will explore a different aspect of Python-based automation, with practical examples and real-world applications to reinforce the material. By the end of this book, you will have gained hands-on experience in automating various systems and workflows using Python, with a solid understanding of AI and machine learning concepts.

Key topics covered in this book include:

- **Automation Basics**: Understanding how automation works, the core principles behind automating tasks, and setting up your Python environment for automation.
- **Python Libraries for Automation**: Learning about essential libraries like pandas, NumPy, Selenium, and others that make automation tasks easier and more efficient.

- **Integrating AI in Automation**: Harnessing the power of AI and machine learning for more intelligent automation. We will cover machine learning models, data preprocessing, and how to integrate AI-driven workflows into automation.

- **Error Handling and Optimization**: Implementing error handling, debugging, and optimizing your Python automation scripts for better performance and reliability.

- **Security and Maintenance**: Understanding how to secure your automation scripts, handle sensitive data, and maintain automated systems over time to ensure they run smoothly.

- **Real-World Applications**: Exploring real-world use cases, such as automating data pipelines, integrating with IoT devices, and automating cloud resource management.

## Why Python for Automation?

Python's popularity in the world of automation stems from its ease of use, readability, and the breadth of its ecosystem. With Python, developers can automate tasks such as:

- **Data extraction, transformation, and loading (ETL)**: Python's libraries, such as **pandas** and **SQLAlchemy**, make it easy to automate data workflows for analysis, reporting, and decision-making.

- **Task Scheduling**: Using Python-based tools like **APScheduler** and **Celery**, automation scripts can be scheduled to run at specific intervals, ensuring that critical tasks such as backups, data syncing, and report generation occur automatically.

- **Web Scraping and Data Collection**: Python excels at web scraping using libraries like **BeautifulSoup** and **Scrapy**, automating the collection of valuable data from websites for analysis or integration into other systems.

- **AI and Machine Learning**: Python is at the forefront of AI and machine learning, with libraries like **TensorFlow**, **PyTorch**, and **Scikit-learn** making it easier to integrate intelligent automation into your workflows, such as predictive analysis, anomaly detection, and decision-making.

- **IoT and Smart Automation**: Python can interface with various IoT devices, enabling automation in areas such as home automation, smart cities, and industrial IoT.

With Python, automation no longer has to be complicated or cumbersome. Its simplicity allows developers to create powerful automation systems that are both scalable and maintainable, enabling them to focus on solving business problems instead of managing complex infrastructure.

## Who This Book Is For:

This book is designed for:

- **Beginners**: Those new to Python programming or automation, looking to understand how to automate simple tasks and progressively move toward more advanced systems.

- **Intermediate Python Developers**: Those with some experience in Python, interested in learning how to integrate automation and AI into their workflows.

- **Data Scientists and Engineers**: Professionals looking to automate data pipelines, machine learning workflows, and ETL processes using Python.

- **AI Enthusiasts**: Anyone interested in applying AI-driven automation solutions to real-world problems, from predictive maintenance to intelligent decision-making systems.

## How to Use This Book:

This book is structured to guide you step-by-step through the various concepts of AI and automation using Python. Each chapter will build on the previous one, introducing new tools and techniques while reinforcing concepts through practical examples.

- **Hands-on Approach**: Each chapter includes hands-on examples that you can try out in your own environment. These examples cover a wide range of automation tasks, from simple data manipulation to integrating machine learning models into workflows.

- **Real-World Use Cases**: Throughout the book, we will dive into real-world use cases, showing how automation is applied in various industries like healthcare, finance, and smart cities, giving you insight into how Python is transforming industries across the globe.

- **Code Examples**: All examples are provided with detailed explanations and code snippets that you can , paste, and modify for your own automation needs.

By the end of this book, you will have the skills necessary to build your own automation systems using Python, integrate AI into your workflows, and optimize processes for increased efficiency. Whether you are automating mundane tasks or designing complex systems, Python is an excellent choice for creating scalable and efficient automation solutions.

Automation is no longer just a buzzword—it's a fundamental component of modern business and technology. As the demand for intelligent, efficient, and scalable solutions grows, Python remains a powerful tool for building and managing automated systems. This book is your gateway to mastering Python-based automation, offering you the tools, techniques, and real-world applications needed to excel in the field.

Let's dive in and begin exploring the power of Python for automation, shaping the future of work and transforming industries along the way.

# Chapter 1: Introduction to AI and Automation with Python

## Understanding AI and Automation

Artificial Intelligence (AI) is one of the most transformative technologies in modern times. It refers to the simulation of human intelligence in machines that are programmed to think, learn, and perform tasks that traditionally required human intervention. AI encompasses a wide range of technologies, including machine learning, natural language processing, and robotics, all of which enable systems to perceive, reason, and act based on data-driven insights. The ultimate goal of AI is to build systems that can perform tasks autonomously, often outperforming humans in terms of speed, accuracy, and efficiency.

Automation, on the other hand, refers to the use of technology to perform tasks with minimal human intervention. It involves the creation of systems that can automatically carry out repetitive, mundane, or complex tasks without the need for constant oversight. While automation has been around for a long time, it has evolved significantly with the advent of AI. AI-powered automation can handle more sophisticated tasks by making intelligent decisions based on real-time data.

In recent years, AI and automation have come together to create systems that not only automate simple, predefined tasks but also adapt and improve over time. These systems are capable of handling dynamic environments, making real-time decisions, and optimizing processes with minimal human input.

### *The Role of AI in Automation*

AI brings a level of sophistication to automation that was previously unimaginable. It enables systems to:

1. **Learn from Data**: Machine learning algorithms, a subset of AI, allow systems to learn from historical data. This means that an automated system can continuously improve its performance based on new information.
2. **Make Predictions**: AI models can predict future trends based on existing data. For instance, a machine learning model can predict customer demand, allowing businesses to automate inventory management or customer service.
3. **Recognize Patterns**: AI systems excel at recognizing patterns in large datasets. For example, AI can automatically categorize images, transcribe speech, or identify fraudulent transactions by recognizing specific patterns that humans may miss.
4. **Adapt to Changes**: Unlike traditional automation systems that follow rigid rules, AI-based automation can adapt to changes in the environment. This makes it ideal for dynamic

scenarios like market fluctuations, customer behavior, or system performance.

AI-driven automation is not only about automating repetitive tasks but also about enhancing decision-making and creating more efficient workflows.

---

## How Python Facilitates AI Tasks

Python has become the programming language of choice for AI and automation for several reasons:

### 1. Simplicity and Readability

Python's clean and readable syntax makes it accessible to both beginners and experts. For AI and automation, this means that developers can focus more on solving problems rather than dealing with complex programming syntax. Python allows developers to write code quickly, experiment with ideas, and refine solutions without worrying about intricate language details.

### 2. Extensive Libraries and Frameworks

Python boasts an impressive range of libraries and frameworks that make AI and automation tasks easier to implement. Some of the most notable libraries include:

- **NumPy**: For numerical computations and working with arrays, which is essential for many AI algorithms.

- **pandas**: For data manipulation and analysis, a cornerstone for any machine learning or automation task.

- **Scikit-learn**: A library for machine learning that includes various algorithms for classification, regression, clustering, and more.

- **TensorFlow and Keras**: For deep learning, providing tools to build, train, and deploy neural networks.

- **NLTK and spaCy**: For natural language processing, including tokenization, text classification, and sentiment analysis.

- **OpenCV**: For computer vision tasks, including image recognition and processing.

- **Selenium**: For automating web browser interactions, making it invaluable for web scraping and testing.

These libraries provide pre-built functions and algorithms that developers can use, significantly reducing the time and effort required to build AI and automation solutions.

### 3. Integration Capabilities

Python's ability to integrate with other technologies, such as databases, web services, and cloud platforms, allows it to serve as the backbone for more extensive automation systems. For instance, Python can connect to cloud storage, pull data from APIs, interact with databases, and trigger automated workflows across various services.

### 4. Support for Big Data and Distributed Computing

Python supports working with big data through libraries like **PySpark** and **Dask**, enabling developers to handle large datasets typically encountered in AI applications. For instance, when training machine learning models, large amounts of data need to be processed efficiently, and Python provides tools to scale the workload across multiple processors or machines.

### 5. Community and Ecosystem

Python has a vast and active community of developers, researchers, and enthusiasts who contribute to its ecosystem. This community-driven approach ensures continuous development of new tools, libraries, and best practices. Whether you are solving a specific AI challenge or building an automation pipeline, Python's community provides resources, tutorials, and support to help you succeed.

---

## Real-World Examples of AI-Driven Automation

### 1. Customer Service Automation

One of the most prominent applications of AI and automation is in customer service. Companies across industries use AI-powered chatbots to interact with customers, providing quick responses to inquiries, troubleshooting issues, and guiding users through complex processes. These chatbots use natural language processing (NLP) techniques to understand and respond to customer queries in real time.

For example, a bank may use an AI chatbot to automate basic customer service tasks such as checking account balances, processing payments, or helping users navigate through services. The chatbot, powered by machine learning, can even adapt over time, improving its responses based on customer interactions.

## 2. Predictive Maintenance in Manufacturing

AI and automation have revolutionized the manufacturing industry by enabling predictive maintenance. Predictive maintenance uses AI algorithms to analyze data from sensors placed on machines and equipment to predict when maintenance is needed. This prevents unexpected breakdowns and reduces downtime.

For instance, in a factory, machines may be equipped with IoT sensors that continuously monitor temperature, vibration, and other variables. AI algorithms process this data in real time, identifying patterns that indicate a machine is likely to fail. The automation system then schedules maintenance, reducing the risk of equipment failure and optimizing operations.

## 3. Robotic Process Automation (RPA) in Finance

Robotic Process Automation (RPA) is another area where AI and automation have made a significant impact. In the financial sector, RPA is used to automate repetitive tasks such as data entry, invoice processing, and transaction reconciliation.

For example, a financial institution may use RPA to process loan applications. The automation system can gather data from various sources, verify the information, and make decisions based on predefined criteria. AI algorithms can then be used to assess the creditworthiness of the applicant, making the entire process faster, more accurate, and less prone to human error.

### 4. AI-Powered Healthcare Diagnostics

In healthcare, AI-driven automation has the potential to improve diagnostics and patient care. For example, AI-powered systems can automatically analyze medical images such as X-rays, MRIs, and CT scans to detect abnormalities like tumors or fractures. These systems use deep learning algorithms to recognize patterns in the images that are often difficult for human radiologists to identify.

In addition to diagnostics, AI can automate administrative tasks like patient scheduling and billing, allowing healthcare professionals to focus more on patient care. For instance, an AI system could automatically schedule appointments based on a patient's condition, availability, and insurance details.

### 5. E-Commerce and Personalized Recommendations

E-commerce platforms like Amazon and Netflix use AI and automation to provide personalized recommendations to their users. These platforms analyze vast amounts of user data, including browsing history, past purchases, and ratings, to generate tailored recommendations.

Python is used extensively in such systems, with machine learning algorithms analyzing user behavior and making predictions about what products or content a user might be interested in. The result is an automated, personalized experience that enhances user satisfaction and drives sales.

### 6. Autonomous Vehicles

Autonomous vehicles, including self-driving cars, rely heavily on AI and automation. These vehicles use sensors and cameras to collect data about their environment, while AI algorithms process this data in real time to make decisions such as navigating roads, detecting obstacles, and obeying traffic rules.

Python plays a crucial role in autonomous vehicle development, with libraries like **TensorFlow** and **Keras** used to train deep learning models for image recognition, and **OpenCV** employed for processing visual data from the car's cameras. The automation system enables vehicles to drive autonomously, potentially transforming the transportation industry.

AI and automation have already begun reshaping industries, improving efficiency, and reducing costs. By combining the power of artificial intelligence with the flexibility of Python, developers can create systems that automate complex tasks and make intelligent decisions. In this chapter, we've explored the fundamental concepts behind AI and automation, highlighting how Python facilitates these technologies and providing real-world examples of their application.

In the chapters that follow, we'll dive deeper into specific techniques and Python libraries that enable AI-driven automation, providing you with the tools and knowledge to build your own automation solutions. Whether you're automating simple tasks or developing sophisticated AI systems, Python offers a robust environment for tackling these challenges.

# Chapter 2: Setting Up Your Python Environment for AI and Automation

## Installing Necessary Libraries and Tools

Before diving into AI and automation projects with Python, it is essential to set up the necessary environment and install the required libraries and tools. In this chapter, we will guide you through the steps to install Python, set up virtual environments, and install essential libraries that are commonly used for AI and automation tasks.

### *Installing Python*

Python is a versatile programming language that supports a wide range of applications, from web development to AI and automation. To get started, you need to install Python on your system.

1. **Download Python**: Visit the official Python website at https://www.python.org/downloads/ and download the latest stable version of Python for your operating system. Python is available for Windows, macOS, and Linux.

2. **Install Python**: Follow the installation instructions for your operating system. During installation on Windows, ensure

that you check the option that says "Add Python to PATH." This makes it easier to use Python from the command line.

3. **Verify Installation**: After installation, open a terminal (or command prompt on Windows) and type the following command to verify that Python is installed correctly:

bash

python --version

If Python is installed correctly, you should see the version number printed in the terminal. For example, Python 3.x.x.

### *Installing Essential Libraries*

Once Python is installed, you need to install libraries that will help you with AI and automation tasks. Python uses a package manager called pip to install these libraries.

1. **Installing pip** (if not already installed): If pip is not installed along with Python (it usually is), you can install it manually by running the following command in the terminal:

bash

python -m ensurepip --upgrade

2. **Common Libraries for AI and Automation**: There are several libraries that are commonly used for AI and automation. Some of the most important ones include:

o **NumPy**: A library for numerical computing in Python, widely used for data manipulation.

bash

```
pip install numpy
```

o **pandas**: A powerful data analysis and manipulation library.

bash

```
pip install pandas
```

o **Scikit-learn**: A library that provides simple tools for machine learning.

bash

```
pip install scikit-learn
```

o **TensorFlow**: A popular deep learning library used for building and training AI models.

bash

```
pip install tensorflow
```

o **Keras**: A high-level neural network library that runs on top of TensorFlow.

bash

pip install keras

- o **Matplotlib and Seaborn**: Libraries for creating visualizations and plots.

bash

pip install matplotlib seaborn

- o **Selenium**: A web automation tool for automating web browsers.

bash

pip install selenium

- o **BeautifulSoup**: A library for web scraping and parsing HTML.

bash

pip install beautifulsoup4

3. These libraries are just the starting point, but they will cover a wide range of tasks related to AI and automation.

## Setting Up Python, Jupyter, and Virtual Environments

While installing libraries globally is fine for simple projects, it is a best practice to use **virtual environments** for isolating your project dependencies. Virtual environments help avoid conflicts between different versions of libraries required by different projects.

### *1. Setting Up a Virtual Environment*

A virtual environment allows you to create isolated Python environments for different projects. This helps you manage project-specific dependencies and ensures that each project uses the correct version of libraries.

1. **Create a Virtual Environment**: To create a virtual environment, open your terminal and navigate to your project directory. Then, run the following command to create a virtual environment:

   bash

   python -m venv myenv
   This command will create a directory named myenv (you can choose any name) containing the virtual environment.

2. **Activate the Virtual Environment**: To start using the virtual environment, you need to activate it:
   - **On Windows**:

bash

myenv\Scripts\activate

- o **On macOS/Linux**:

bash

source myenv/bin/activate

3. After activation, you should see the name of the virtual environment in the terminal prompt, indicating that it is active.

4. **Deactivating the Virtual Environment**: When you are done with your work in the virtual environment, you can deactivate it by running:

bash

deactivate

5. **Installing Libraries in the Virtual Environment**: With the virtual environment activated, you can now install the necessary libraries using pip without affecting the global Python environment:

bash

pip install numpy pandas scikit-learn tensorflow

*2. Installing Jupyter Notebooks*

Jupyter Notebooks are a great tool for developing and testing AI and automation code interactively. They allow you to write and execute code in small chunks, visualize data, and document your process.

1. **Installing Jupyter**: To install Jupyter, first ensure that you have activated your virtual environment. Then, run the following command:

   bash

   pip install jupyter

2. **Running Jupyter Notebook**: Once installed, you can start a Jupyter Notebook session by running:

   bash

   jupyter notebook

   This will open a new tab in your default web browser, where you can create and work on notebooks interactively.

---

# Example: A Simple Python Script for Automation

Now that we have the environment set up, let's write a simple Python script that demonstrates basic automation. This script will download a webpage and extract all the links from it using the **requests** and **BeautifulSoup** libraries.

1. **Install the Required Libraries**: If you haven't installed requests and beautifulsoup4, run the following command in your terminal:

bash

pip install requests beautifulsoup4

2. **Write the Python Script**: Create a Python file, say web_scraper.py, and open it in your preferred code editor. Add the following code:

python

```python
import requests
from bs4 import BeautifulSoup

# Function to fetch all links from a webpage
def fetch_links(url):
    # Send a GET request to the URL
    response = requests.get(url)

    # Check if the request was successful
    if response.status_code == 200:
        # Parse the HTML content using BeautifulSoup
        soup = BeautifulSoup(response.text, 'html.parser')
```

```python
# Find all anchor tags (<a>) and extract their href attributes
links = soup.find_all('a', href=True)

# Print the links
for link in links:
    print(link['href'])
    else:
    print("Failed to retrieve the webpage.")

# Test the function
if __name__ == "__main__":
    fetch_links('https://www.example.com')
```

3. **Run the Script**: Save the file and run it using Python from the terminal:

bash

```bash
python web_scraper.py
```

If successful, the script will print out all the links found on the webpage https://www.example.com.

---

In this chapter, we've covered the essential steps for setting up your Python environment for AI and automation projects. From installing Python and libraries to creating virtual environments and running

Jupyter Notebooks, you've learned how to prepare your system for working with AI tools and automation frameworks.

The simple Python script for automation that we explored demonstrates how easy it is to automate tasks using Python. In the following chapters, we'll dive deeper into more advanced concepts, exploring how Python can help automate complex workflows, build machine learning models, and create sophisticated AI applications.

# Chapter 3: The Basics of Python for Automation

---

## Core Python Concepts for Automation

Python is one of the most accessible programming languages, making it ideal for automation tasks. It is well-suited for automating repetitive tasks due to its simple syntax and readability. In this chapter, we will cover some essential Python concepts that form the foundation for writing automation scripts. These concepts are crucial for building efficient, scalable, and maintainable automation workflows.

### *Variables and Data Types*

Python supports various data types, such as strings, integers, floats, lists, dictionaries, tuples, and sets. Understanding how to use and manipulate these data types is key to automating tasks.

- **String**: A sequence of characters used for text manipulation.
- **Integer**: Whole numbers used for counting and calculations.
- **Float**: Numbers with decimals used for precise calculations.
- **List**: A mutable collection of ordered items, ideal for storing multiple values.

- **Dictionary**: A collection of key-value pairs, useful for associating values with keys.
- **Tuple**: An immutable collection of items that cannot be modified after creation.
- **Set**: A collection of unique values, often used to eliminate duplicates.

Example of variables:

python

```
name = "John Doe"
age = 30
height = 5.9
fruits = ["apple", "banana", "cherry"]
person = {"name": "John", "age": 30}
```

Understanding these data types and knowing when to use them is essential for writing effective automation scripts.

### *Operators*

Python includes a variety of operators that allow you to perform operations on variables. These include:

- **Arithmetic Operators**: Used for mathematical operations like addition, subtraction, multiplication, etc.
  - +, -, *, /, //, %, **
- **Comparison Operators**: Used to compare values.
  - ==, !=, >, <, >=, <=

- **Logical Operators**: Used to combine conditional statements.
  - and, or, not

## *Working with Files*

One of the most common tasks in automation is interacting with files. Python provides built-in functions to read from and write to files. You can open files using the open() function, and you can read, write, or append data using methods like read(), write(), and writelines().

Example of reading a file:

python

```
with open('example.txt', 'r') as file:
    content = file.read()
    print(content)
```

This basic understanding of Python data types, operators, and file handling will provide the foundation for automating tasks such as data processing, file manipulation, and system administration.

---

## **Functions, Loops, and Conditionals in Automation Tasks**

In Python, functions, loops, and conditionals are the building blocks for writing automation scripts. Let's dive deeper into each of these concepts and how they apply to automation.

## *Functions*

A function is a block of code that only runs when called. Functions are reusable, making them ideal for automating tasks that need to be performed multiple times.

- **Defining a Function**: You define a function using the def keyword, followed by the function name and parameters.
- **Calling a Function**: Once a function is defined, you can call it whenever necessary.

Example:

python

```
def greet(name):
    print(f"Hello, {name}!")

greet("John")
greet("Alice")
```

**Why Functions Are Important for Automation**: Functions allow you to modularize your code, making it more maintainable and readable. If you have a repetitive task, placing it inside a function makes your automation script more concise and reusable.

## *Loops*

Loops allow you to execute a block of code multiple times. Python has two primary types of loops: for loops and while loops. Loops are particularly useful when automating tasks that involve processing multiple items.

- **For Loop**: Iterates over a sequence (like a list, tuple, or string) and executes the code inside the loop for each item.

Example:

python

```
fruits = ["apple", "banana", "cherry"]
for fruit in fruits:
    print(fruit)
```

- **While Loop**: Repeats the block of code as long as the specified condition is True.

Example:

python

```
counter = 0
while counter < 5:
    print(f"Counter is: {counter}")
    counter += 1
```

**Why Loops Are Important for Automation**: Loops enable you to automate tasks like batch processing, repetitive data analysis, or checking multiple conditions in a system. For example, a loop can automate the process of renaming files in a directory or processing items in a queue.

### *Conditionals*

Conditional statements in Python are used to make decisions in your code. The most common conditional statements are if, elif, and else. These statements help determine the flow of the program based on certain conditions.

Example:

python

```
age = 18
if age >= 18:
    print("You are an adult.")
else:
    print("You are a minor.")
```

**Why Conditionals Are Important for Automation**: Conditional statements allow your automation scripts to make decisions based on specific conditions. For instance, if you're automating the process of sending emails, you can use conditionals to check whether a user is subscribed to a newsletter before sending the email.

---

## Example: Automating a File Renaming Task

Let's now combine everything we've learned to automate a simple file renaming task. Imagine you have a folder full of images, and you want to rename all the files in that folder to include a timestamp.

*Steps:*

1. **Navigate through a folder** and list all the files.

2. **Check if the file is an image** (e.g., .jpg, .png).

3. **Rename each file** by adding a timestamp to the filename.

## *Solution:*

python

```python
import os
from datetime import datetime

def rename_files_in_directory(directory_path):
    # Get the list of files in the specified directory
    files = os.listdir(directory_path)

    # Loop through all files
    for file in files:
        # Check if the file is an image (i.e., ends with .jpg or .png)
        if file.endswith('.jpg') or file.endswith('.png'):
            # Get the current timestamp
            timestamp = datetime.now().strftime('%Y%m%d_%H%M%S')

            # Construct the new filename with the timestamp
            new_name = f"{timestamp}_{file}"

            # Construct the full file path
            old_path = os.path.join(directory_path, file)
            new_path = os.path.join(directory_path, new_name)

            # Rename the file
            os.rename(old_path, new_path)
```

```
        print(f"Renamed: {file} to {new_name}")
    else:
        print(f"Skipped: {file} (not an image file)")


# Example usage
directory = '/path/to/your/directory'
rename_files_in_directory(directory)
```

## *How It Works:*

1. **Listing Files**: The script uses the os.listdir() function to get a list of all files in the specified directory.

2. **Checking File Type**: It then checks whether each file is an image by examining its extension.

3. **Renaming Files**: For each image file, the script generates a new filename using the current timestamp, which is formatted as YYYYMMDD_HHMMSS. The file is then renamed using the os.rename() function.

4. **Skipping Non-Image Files**: The script skips files that do not match the specified image extensions (.jpg or .png).

## *Example Output:*

bash

```
Renamed: photo1.jpg to 20250117_123456_photo1.jpg
Renamed: photo2.png to 20250117_123457_photo2.png
Skipped: document.txt (not an image file)
```

In this chapter, we've covered some of the core Python concepts essential for automation tasks, including variables, functions, loops, and conditionals. We've also demonstrated how to use these concepts to automate a file renaming task, which is a common use case in automation workflows.

By mastering these fundamental concepts, you will be well-equipped to automate a wide range of tasks, from simple file manipulation to more complex data processing and system management. As we move forward, we will explore more advanced automation techniques and workflows, leveraging Python's rich ecosystem of libraries and tools.

# Chapter 4: Python Libraries for AI and Automation

---

## Introduction to Popular Libraries: NumPy, pandas, Scikit-learn

Python's ecosystem is rich with powerful libraries that can help you accomplish a wide variety of tasks in AI and automation. In this chapter, we'll explore some of the most popular libraries in Python used for AI, machine learning, data manipulation, and automation.

### *1. NumPy: Numerical Computing for AI and Automation*

**NumPy** is the foundational library for numerical computing in Python. It provides support for arrays and matrices, as well as a collection of mathematical functions to manipulate these structures. NumPy is critical for AI tasks as it enables efficient handling of large datasets and numerical computations, which are common in machine learning and data analysis.

- **Core Features**:
  - **N-dimensional arrays**: NumPy introduces the ndarray data type, a multi-dimensional array that allows for fast operations on large datasets.

- o **Mathematical functions**: NumPy provides many built-in mathematical functions, such as sum(), mean(), std(), and dot().

- o **Linear algebra**: NumPy supports linear algebra operations, such as matrix multiplication and determinant calculation, which are essential in many AI algorithms.

**Example**:

python

import numpy as np

# Create a 2D NumPy array
array = np.array([[1, 2, 3], [4, 5, 6]])

# Perform element-wise addition
result = array + 10
print(result)

## 2. pandas: Data Manipulation and Analysis

**pandas** is a powerful library used for data manipulation and analysis. It provides two primary data structures, DataFrame and Series, that make it easy to handle, analyze, and manipulate structured data (e.g., CSV files, SQL databases, etc.). pandas is essential when automating data preprocessing, cleaning, and analysis.

- **Core Features**:
  - o **DataFrames**: A DataFrame is a two-dimensional data structure with labeled axes, making it perfect for handling structured data.
  - o **Data selection and filtering**: pandas allows you to select rows and columns easily, filter data, and perform aggregations.
  - o **Time series support**: pandas includes powerful tools for handling time series data, which is often necessary for automating tasks like stock price analysis or sensor data processing.

**Example**:

python

```
import pandas as pd

# Create a DataFrame
data = {'Name': ['Alice', 'Bob', 'Charlie'], 'Age': [25, 30, 35]}
df = pd.DataFrame(data)

# Filter rows where age is greater than 28
filtered_data = df[df['Age'] > 28]
print(filtered_data)
```

### 3. Scikit-learn: Machine Learning for Automation

**Scikit-learn** is one of the most popular libraries for machine learning in Python. It provides simple and efficient tools for data mining and data analysis, and it is built on top of NumPy and pandas. Scikit-learn is essential for AI and automation tasks that involve building predictive models, performing classification and regression, and conducting clustering.

- **Core Features**:
  - **Preprocessing**: Scikit-learn provides tools for scaling, normalizing, and encoding data.
  - **Classification and regression**: It includes implementations of common machine learning algorithms, such as decision trees, logistic regression, and support vector machines.
  - **Clustering and dimensionality reduction**: It offers tools for unsupervised learning, like k-means clustering and principal component analysis (PCA).

**Example**:

python

```
from sklearn.datasets import load_iris
from sklearn.model_selection import train_test_split
from sklearn.ensemble import RandomForestClassifier

# Load the Iris dataset
iris = load_iris()
```

```
X, y = iris.data, iris.target

# Split the dataset into training and test sets
X_train, X_test, y_train, y_test = train_test_split(X, y, test_size=0.2)

# Train a Random Forest model
model = RandomForestClassifier()
model.fit(X_train, y_train)

# Evaluate the model's performance
score = model.score(X_test, y_test)
print(f"Accuracy: {score * 100:.2f}%")
```

---

# Libraries for Web Scraping, Task Scheduling, and Automation

Python is also equipped with a variety of libraries designed specifically for web scraping, task scheduling, and general automation tasks. These libraries enable you to automate workflows such as data collection, interacting with websites, and executing tasks at scheduled intervals.

## 1. Web Scraping with BeautifulSoup and Requests

Web scraping is the process of extracting data from websites. Python offers several libraries for web scraping, but **BeautifulSoup** (for parsing HTML) and **requests** (for sending HTTP requests) are the most commonly used.

- **requests**: A simple HTTP library for making requests to web pages and APIs. It allows you to send GET or POST requests to retrieve data from a website.
- **BeautifulSoup**: A library used for parsing HTML and XML documents. It allows you to search the document, extract elements, and navigate through the HTML structure.

## Example: Automating Data Collection Using Requests and BeautifulSoup

Let's automate the process of scraping headlines from a news website. In this example, we will use **requests** to retrieve the webpage and **BeautifulSoup** to extract the headlines.

**Installation**:

bash

pip install requests beautifulsoup4

**Script**:

python

```
import requests
from bs4 import BeautifulSoup

# Send an HTTP GET request to the website
url = 'https://www.bbc.com'
response = requests.get(url)
```

```python
# Check if the request was successful
if response.status_code == 200:
    # Parse the content of the page with BeautifulSoup
    soup = BeautifulSoup(response.text, 'html.parser')

    # Find all headline tags (e.g., h3) and extract the text
    headlines = soup.find_all('h3')

    # Print each headline
    for headline in headlines:
        print(headline.text.strip())
else:
    print("Failed to retrieve the webpage.")
```

## 2. Task Scheduling with schedule

Python's **schedule** library makes it easy to schedule tasks to run at specific intervals, such as every hour, day, or week.

- **schedule**: A simple-to-use library for scheduling periodic tasks. It allows you to set up tasks to be executed at regular intervals, like running a script every morning or checking a server's status every hour.

### Example: Automating Tasks with schedule

Let's automate a task that prints a message every 10 seconds.

### Installation:

bash

pip install schedule

**Script**:

python

```
import schedule
import time

def job():
    print("This task runs every 10 seconds.")

# Schedule the job to run every 10 seconds
schedule.every(10).seconds.do(job)

# Keep the script running and check for pending tasks
while True:
    schedule.run_pending()
    time.sleep(1)
```

In this example, the job() function is scheduled to run every 10 seconds. The while loop keeps the script running, checking for pending tasks.

### 3. Automating System Tasks with os and subprocess

Python also includes built-in libraries like os and subprocess for automating system-level tasks. These libraries allow you to interact with the operating system, run shell commands, manage files, and handle processes.

- **os**: Provides functions for interacting with the operating system, such as creating files and directories or modifying file paths.

- **subprocess**: Allows you to run shell commands and interact with the system shell.

## Example: Running a System Command

python

```
import subprocess

# Run a system command (e.g., list files in the current directory)
subprocess.run(["ls", "-l"])
```

This example uses subprocess.run() to execute the ls -l command, which lists files in the current directory.

In this chapter, we have explored some of the essential Python libraries for AI and automation, including **NumPy, pandas**, and **Scikit-learn** for data manipulation and machine learning, as well as libraries like **requests, BeautifulSoup**, and **schedule** for web scraping and task automation.

By understanding how to use these libraries effectively, you can build powerful automation systems for a wide range of tasks, from data collection and processing to machine learning and system administration. As you progress, you'll be able to integrate these tools into more complex automation workflows, reducing the need for manual intervention and increasing efficiency across various processes.

In the next chapters, we will dive deeper into real-world automation examples and explore advanced techniques for scaling your automation systems.

# Chapter 5: Introduction to Machine Learning for Automation

## Understanding Machine Learning Basics

Machine Learning (ML) is a subset of Artificial Intelligence (AI) that focuses on building systems that can learn from data and make predictions or decisions based on it, without being explicitly programmed to perform specific tasks. ML enables automation by allowing systems to improve and adapt through experience, making it an essential tool for creating intelligent and efficient automation systems.

At its core, machine learning involves training a model on a set of data, allowing it to make predictions, detect patterns, or categorize new data based on what it has learned. ML algorithms can be broadly classified into three categories: supervised learning, unsupervised learning, and reinforcement learning. In this chapter, we will focus on supervised and unsupervised learning, as they are the most commonly used techniques in automation tasks.

### How Machine Learning Works

Machine learning typically involves the following steps:

1. **Data Collection**: Collecting relevant and high-quality data, which will be used to train the machine learning model. The data can be anything from numerical values to images or text.

2. **Data Preprocessing**: Cleaning and preparing the data for the model. This can involve handling missing values, normalizing the data, encoding categorical variables, and splitting the data into training and testing sets.

3. **Model Selection**: Choosing an appropriate machine learning algorithm or model based on the problem type (e.g., regression, classification, clustering).

4. **Training the Model**: Feeding the prepared data into the model, which "learns" the patterns and relationships between the features (inputs) and the target (output).

5. **Evaluation**: Evaluating the model's performance using metrics like accuracy, precision, recall, or mean squared error, depending on the problem.

6. **Prediction and Deployment**: Once the model is trained and validated, it can be deployed to make predictions or automate tasks on new data.

### *Common Machine Learning Algorithms*

- **Linear Regression**: A statistical method for predicting a continuous target variable based on one or more features.

- **Logistic Regression**: Used for binary classification problems (e.g., yes/no, true/false).

- **Decision Trees**: A hierarchical model used for classification and regression tasks.
- **Random Forests**: An ensemble method that combines multiple decision trees to improve prediction accuracy.
- **Support Vector Machines (SVM)**: A supervised learning algorithm used for classification tasks by finding a hyperplane that separates classes.
- **K-Means Clustering**: An unsupervised learning algorithm used for grouping similar data points into clusters.

Machine learning has become indispensable in automation, particularly for tasks like predictive maintenance, demand forecasting, anomaly detection, and more.

## Supervised vs. Unsupervised Learning

The two primary types of machine learning are **supervised learning** and **unsupervised learning**. Each of these methods is suitable for different types of automation problems.

### Supervised Learning

Supervised learning is the most common type of machine learning, where the model is trained on labeled data. Labeled data means that the dataset includes both the input features (data) and the corresponding correct output (label or target).

- **How it works**: The model learns from the labeled training data by identifying patterns or relationships between the input features and the target. Once trained, it can predict the target value for new, unseen data.
- **Examples of Supervised Learning Problems**:
  - **Classification**: Predicting a discrete label or class, such as identifying whether an email is spam or not.
  - **Regression**: Predicting a continuous value, such as predicting the price of a house based on features like size and location.

**Popular Supervised Learning Algorithms**:

- Linear Regression
- Logistic Regression
- Decision Trees
- Random Forests
- Support Vector Machines

**Example of Supervised Learning**: A spam email classifier, where the model is trained on labeled emails (spam or not spam) and then used to classify new emails as spam or not.

*Unsupervised Learning*

Unsupervised learning, on the other hand, deals with data that has no labels. The model is given only the input features and must find patterns, structure, or relationships within the data on its own.

- **How it works**: Unsupervised learning algorithms identify hidden patterns or groupings within the data, such as clustering similar data points or reducing the dimensions of the data.
- **Examples of Unsupervised Learning Problems**:
  - ○ **Clustering**: Grouping data into clusters, such as customer segmentation based on purchase behavior.
  - ○ **Dimensionality Reduction**: Reducing the number of features in a dataset while preserving important information, such as using Principal Component Analysis (PCA) to reduce the dimensionality of large datasets.

**Popular Unsupervised Learning Algorithms**:

- K-Means Clustering
- Hierarchical Clustering
- Principal Component Analysis (PCA)

**Example of Unsupervised Learning**: Customer segmentation, where the model groups customers into different clusters based on their purchase history.

---

# Example: Automating Predictions with Machine Learning Models

In this section, we'll walk through an example of how to automate predictions using a machine learning model. Let's consider a simple scenario where we want to predict whether a customer will churn (leave) or stay with a company based on certain customer data, such as age, subscription type, and usage.

We will use a supervised learning approach, specifically a **Random Forest Classifier**, to build our model.

*Steps:*

1. **Install Required Libraries**: First, you need to install the required libraries: pandas, numpy, scikit-learn, and matplotlib for visualization.

   bash

   ```bash
   pip install pandas numpy scikit-learn matplotlib
   ```

2. **Load and Prepare Data**: We'll use a fictional dataset that contains customer information and whether they have churned or not. The data might look something like this:

   python

   ```python
   import pandas as pd
   from sklearn.model_selection import train_test_split
   from sklearn.ensemble import RandomForestClassifier
   from sklearn.metrics import accuracy_score
   ```

```
import matplotlib.pyplot as plt

# Load the dataset
data = pd.read_csv('customer_churn.csv')

# Example dataset columns: Age, Subscription_Type, Usage, Churn (1
= yes, 0 = no)
print(data.head())
```

3. **Preprocess the Data**: Before training the model, we need to preprocess the data. This involves handling missing values, converting categorical variables into numerical values, and splitting the data into training and testing sets.

python

```
# Fill missing values (if any)
data.fillna(method='ffill', inplace=True)

# Convert categorical data to numerical (if necessary)
data['Subscription_Type'] = data['Subscription_Type'].map({'Basic': 0,
'Premium': 1})

# Split the data into features (X) and target (y)
X = data[['Age', 'Subscription_Type', 'Usage']]  # Features
y = data['Churn']  # Target

# Split the data into training and testing sets
X_train, X_test, y_train, y_test = train_test_split(X, y, test_size=0.3,
random_state=42)
```

4. **Train the Model**: Now, let's train the **Random Forest Classifier** model using the training data.

python

```
# Initialize the Random Forest Classifier
model = RandomForestClassifier(n_estimators=100, random_state=42)

# Train the model on the training data
model.fit(X_train, y_train)
```

5. **Make Predictions**: After training the model, we can use it to make predictions on the test data.

python

```
# Make predictions on the test data
y_pred = model.predict(X_test)

# Evaluate the model's accuracy
accuracy = accuracy_score(y_test, y_pred)
print(f'Accuracy: {accuracy * 100:.2f}%')
```

6. **Visualizing Feature Importance**: One of the advantages of using a Random Forest model is that it provides insights into which features are most important for making predictions. We can visualize this with a bar plot.

python

```
# Plot feature importance
feature_importance = model.feature_importances_
features = X.columns
plt.bar(features, feature_importance)
plt.title('Feature Importance')
plt.xlabel('Features')
plt.ylabel('Importance')
plt.show()
```

### *of Example:*

In this example, we demonstrated how to automate the prediction of customer churn using a Random Forest Classifier. The process included data preprocessing, training a machine learning model, and evaluating its performance. The model's predictions can be used to automate tasks such as identifying at-risk customers and triggering retention campaigns.

---

In this chapter, we've explored the basics of machine learning, focusing on supervised and unsupervised learning. We discussed key concepts such as classification, regression, clustering, and dimensionality reduction, and provided examples of when and how these techniques are applied in automation scenarios.

The example of automating customer churn prediction using a Random Forest Classifier illustrated how machine learning models can be used to automate decision-making processes, ultimately making systems smarter and more efficient. As you continue building automation systems, incorporating machine learning will allow you to handle more complex tasks, such as predicting outcomes, detecting anomalies, and clustering data for better insights.

In the next chapters, we will dive deeper into more advanced machine learning techniques and their applications in automation.

# Chapter 6: Data Preprocessing for AI

## Techniques for Cleaning and Preparing Data

Data preprocessing is a crucial step in any machine learning or AI pipeline, as the quality and format of the data directly impact the performance of the models. Real-world data is often messy, incomplete, and inconsistent, and to make it usable for training machine learning models, it must be cleaned and transformed. This chapter will cover various techniques for cleaning and preparing data for AI tasks, focusing on handling missing values, scaling data, and encoding categorical variables.

### 1. Importance of Data Preprocessing

Data preprocessing involves transforming raw data into a format that is suitable for analysis or model training. Effective preprocessing helps the model learn efficiently, avoid overfitting, and make accurate predictions. Without proper preprocessing, machine learning models may underperform or fail to produce useful results.

### 2. Common Data Preprocessing Tasks

The following are key tasks involved in data preprocessing:

- **Data Cleaning**: Identifying and correcting errors or inconsistencies in the dataset.

- **Handling Missing Data**: Dealing with gaps in the data, either by imputing values or removing missing records.

- **Scaling Data**: Normalizing or standardizing numerical features to bring them to the same scale.

- **Encoding Categorical Variables**: Converting non-numeric categories (such as "Male" or "Female") into numeric values that the model can understand.

- **Feature Engineering**: Creating new features or transforming existing ones to improve model performance.

Let's go deeper into these tasks and explore the techniques used to carry them out.

---

## Handling Missing Values

Missing values are a common problem in real-world datasets. Whether it's due to errors during data collection, missing entries, or data extraction issues, handling these gaps is crucial for building a reliable machine learning model. There are several techniques for dealing with missing data, depending on the context and nature of the dataset.

### *1. Removing Missing Data*

One simple approach is to remove rows or columns with missing values. However, this is only recommended when the proportion of missing data is small, as it may result in the loss of valuable information.

- **Remove Rows**: You can remove rows where any value is missing.
- **Remove Columns**: If a particular column has a lot of missing values, removing the entire column might be appropriate.

**Example**:

python

import pandas as pd

```
# Load the data
data = pd.read_csv('sales_data.csv')

# Remove rows with missing values
data_cleaned = data.dropna(axis=0)  # Axis 0 is for rows

# Remove columns with missing values
data_cleaned = data.dropna(axis=1)  # Axis 1 is for columns
```

## 2. Imputation

Imputation refers to filling in the missing values with some calculated values, such as the mean, median, or mode for numerical data or the most frequent category for categorical data. Imputation helps retain the dataset's size while making it complete.

- **Numerical Data**: You can replace missing numerical values with the mean or median of the column.
- **Categorical Data**: Missing values in categorical columns can be imputed with the mode (the most frequent category).

**Example**:

python

from sklearn.impute import SimpleImputer

```
# Impute missing values with the mean for numerical columns
imputer = SimpleImputer(strategy='mean')
data_cleaned                                                    =
pd.DataFrame(imputer.fit_transform(data.select_dtypes(include=['float64',
'int64'])))

# For categorical columns, impute missing values with the mode
categorical_imputer = SimpleImputer(strategy='most_frequent')
data_cleaned[categorical_columns]                               =
categorical_imputer.fit_transform(data[categorical_columns])
```

## Scaling Data

Scaling is essential when working with machine learning models that rely on the magnitude of features. Models such as **K-Nearest Neighbors**, **Logistic Regression**, and **Support Vector Machines** are sensitive to the scale of input features, and features with large ranges can dominate the learning process. Scaling ensures that all features are on a comparable scale, which can improve model performance.

There are two primary techniques for scaling data:

### 1. Normalization (Min-Max Scaling)

Normalization scales the data to a fixed range, typically [0, 1]. It is useful when the data has varying units or ranges and needs to be brought into a uniform scale. The formula for normalization is:

$$X\_norm = \frac{X - X_{min}}{X_{max} - X_{min}}$$

**Example**:

python

```
from sklearn.preprocessing import MinMaxScaler

# Apply Min-Max Scaling
scaler = MinMaxScaler()
data_normalized = pd.DataFrame(scaler.fit_transform(data[numerical_columns]))
```

### 2. Standardization (Z-Score Scaling)

Standardization transforms the data so that it has a mean of 0 and a standard deviation of 1. This method is ideal when you want to preserve the distribution of the data but standardize its scale. The formula for standardization is:

$$\text{X\_standardized} = \frac{X - \mu}{\sigma}$$

Where $\mu$ is the mean and $\sigma$ is the standard deviation.

**Example**:

python

```
from sklearn.preprocessing import StandardScaler

# Apply Standardization
scaler = StandardScaler()
data_standardized = pd.DataFrame(scaler.fit_transform(data[numerical_columns]))
```

## Encoding Categorical Variables

Many machine learning algorithms, such as **Linear Regression, Random Forests**, and **Support Vector Machines**, require input data to be numerical. Categorical variables, such as "color" or "product type," need to be encoded into numerical values before they can be used in the model.

### *1. Label Encoding*

Label encoding is the simplest method, where each category in a feature is assigned a unique integer. However, it is more suitable for ordinal data (where there is a meaningful order between categories).

**Example**:

python

```
from sklearn.preprocessing import LabelEncoder

# Encode categorical data using Label Encoding
label_encoder = LabelEncoder()
data['category_encoded'] = label_encoder.fit_transform(data['category_column'])
```

### *2. One-Hot Encoding*

One-hot encoding is used for nominal (non-ordinal) categorical variables. It converts each category into a binary vector, where only one element is 1 (indicating the category), and the rest are 0. This ensures that there is no ordinal relationship between the categories.

**Example**:

python

```
# Apply One-Hot Encoding
data_encoded    =    pd.get_dummies(data,    columns=['category_column'],
drop_first=True)
```

The drop_first=True option avoids creating an extra binary column that would lead to multicollinearity in models.

# Example: Preprocessing Real-World Sales Data for Automation

In this example, we will preprocess a real-world sales dataset for automation. The dataset contains customer details, sales values, and product types, with some missing values and categorical columns that need encoding.

### Step 1: Load the Data
python

```
import pandas as pd

# Load the sales data
sales_data = pd.read_csv('sales_data.csv')
```

### Step 2: Handle Missing Values
First, let's handle missing values by imputing the numerical columns with the median and categorical columns with the mode.

python

```
from sklearn.impute import SimpleImputer

# Impute missing numerical data with median
numerical_imputer = SimpleImputer(strategy='median')
sales_data[['age', 'income', 'sales_value']] = numerical_imputer.fit_transform(sales_data[['age', 'income', 'sales_value']])
```

```
# Impute missing categorical data with the mode
categorical_imputer = SimpleImputer(strategy='most_frequent')
sales_data[['product_type']]                                    =
categorical_imputer.fit_transform(sales_data[['product_type']])
```

### Step 3: Scale the Numerical Data

We will standardize the numerical columns (age, income, sales_value) to have a mean of 0 and a standard deviation of 1.

python

```
from sklearn.preprocessing import StandardScaler

# Apply standardization to the numerical columns
scaler = StandardScaler()
sales_data[['age', 'income', 'sales_value']] = scaler.fit_transform(sales_data[['age', 'income', 'sales_value']])
```

### Step 4: Encode the Categorical Data

We'll use one-hot encoding to encode the product_type column.

python

```
# Apply one-hot encoding to the 'product_type' column
sales_data_encoded = pd.get_dummies(sales_data, columns=['product_type'], drop_first=True)
```

### Step 5: Final Preprocessed Data

At this point, the data is cleaned, scaled, and ready for use in a machine learning model.

python

```
# View the preprocessed data
print(sales_data_encoded.head())
```

---

In this chapter, we've explored the essential techniques for preprocessing data for AI tasks. These techniques, including handling missing values, scaling numerical data, and encoding categorical variables, are critical for ensuring that your data is in a format suitable for machine learning models.

We walked through a real-world example of preprocessing sales data, where we cleaned the data, handled missing values, scaled numerical features, and encoded categorical variables. With properly preprocessed data, we can proceed to build and train machine learning models that can automate tasks such as sales forecasting, customer segmentation, and product recommendation.

Data preprocessing is a key skill in AI and automation, as the quality of your data will directly impact the success of your automation system. As we move forward, we will continue to explore advanced data processing techniques and how to leverage them to create powerful AI-driven automation systems.

# Chapter 7: Working with APIs for Automation

---

## Introduction to APIs and How to Use Them with Python

APIs (Application Programming Interfaces) play a pivotal role in automating workflows and integrating external systems into your applications. An API allows different software systems to communicate with each other, enabling you to send and receive data from a server or third-party service. APIs have become a fundamental tool for accessing online resources such as weather data, financial information, user data, and much more.

Python provides a range of tools to work with APIs, and the most commonly used library for interacting with APIs is **requests**. This library simplifies the process of sending HTTP requests, handling responses, and parsing data from APIs.

### *How APIs Work*

APIs work by providing a set of predefined endpoints (URLs) that you can query. These endpoints accept parameters that define the request and return data, usually in formats like **JSON** or **XML**. The general flow of working with an API looks like this:

1. **Make a Request**: You send a request to an API endpoint, usually over HTTP (GET, POST, PUT, DELETE).
2. **Receive the Response**: The server processes the request and returns data, typically in JSON or XML format.
3. **Parse the Data**: The data returned by the API is parsed so you can work with it in your program.
4. **Handle the Data**: Once the data is parsed, you can use it to automate tasks, such as storing it in a database, displaying it in a dashboard, or making further calculations.

Python's **requests** library simplifies this process by providing an easy-to-use interface for sending HTTP requests and handling responses.

## Authentication and Data Requests

When working with APIs, especially those providing sensitive data or services, authentication is often required. Authentication ensures that only authorized users can access certain API endpoints. There are several methods of authentication, depending on the API:

### *1. API Key Authentication*
Many APIs require you to include an API key in your request. The API key is a unique identifier assigned to your application and allows the server to recognize and authenticate your requests.

To use an API key, you typically include it in the headers or as a query parameter in your request.

**Example (using API key in headers)**:

python

```
import requests

# Define the API endpoint and API key
url = 'https://api.example.com/data'
headers = {'Authorization': 'Bearer YOUR_API_KEY'}

# Send a GET request to the API
response = requests.get(url, headers=headers)

# Check if the request was successful
if response.status_code == 200:
    data = response.json()  # Parse JSON response
    print(data)
else:
    print(f"Failed to retrieve data: {response.status_code}")
```

## 2. OAuth Authentication

OAuth is a more secure and flexible authentication protocol used by APIs that require user access. It allows you to authenticate without exposing user credentials by obtaining an access token.

**OAuth 2.0** is the most common version, and it involves obtaining an authorization code, exchanging it for an access token, and using that token in subsequent API requests.

Here's a simplified flow:

- You authenticate via a login page (handled by the OAuth provider).
- You receive an authorization code, which you exchange for an access token.
- You use the access token to make API requests.

OAuth can be a more complex setup compared to API key authentication but is often used for APIs that require user consent and access to private data.

---

## Example: Automating Data Retrieval from a Weather API

In this example, we will automate the retrieval of weather data from an external API. We will use a weather API (e.g., OpenWeatherMap or WeatherAPI) that provides real-time weather information for a specified location. We'll cover the process of sending a request, handling the response, and automating the retrieval of weather data.

### Step 1: Sign Up for an API Key

To access weather data, you'll need an API key from a weather service. For this example, we will use **OpenWeatherMap**. You can sign up for a free API key at https://openweathermap.org/api.

### Step 2: Install the Requests Library

If you haven't already installed the **requests** library, you can do so by running the following command:

bash

```
pip install requests
```

### Step 3: Make the API Request

Once you have the API key, you can use it to retrieve weather data by sending a **GET** request to the weather API. We'll automate the retrieval of weather data for a specific city.

Here's how you can send the request and handle the response:

python

```
import requests

# Define the API endpoint and parameters
API_KEY = 'YOUR_API_KEY'  # Replace with your API key
city = 'London'  # City for which to get the weather
url                                              =
f'http://api.openweathermap.org/data/2.5/weather?q={city}&appid={API_KEY}
&units=metric'
```

```python
# Send a GET request to the API
response = requests.get(url)

# Check if the request was successful
if response.status_code == 200:
    # Parse the JSON response
    data = response.json()

    # Extract relevant weather information
    city_name = data['name']
    temperature = data['main']['temp']
    description = data['weather'][0]['description']

    # Print the weather information
    print(f"Weather in {city_name}:")
    print(f"Temperature: {temperature}°C")
    print(f"Description: {description}")
else:
    print(f"Failed to retrieve data: {response.status_code}")
```

## *Explanation:*

- **URL Construction**: The URL is dynamically constructed by inserting the city name and your API key. The units=metric parameter ensures that the temperature is returned in Celsius.
- **Sending the Request**: The requests.get(url) sends the GET request to the API.
- **Parsing the Response**: The response is in JSON format, so we parse it using response.json().

- **Extracting Data**: We extract the city name, temperature, and weather description from the JSON response and print them.

### Step 4: Automating the Task

To automate the retrieval of weather data, you can set up a script that runs at regular intervals (e.g., every hour) using Python's **schedule** library.

bash

```
pip install schedule
```

Here's how you can automate the data retrieval:

python

```
import schedule
import time

def get_weather():
    # Define the API request as before
    API_KEY = 'YOUR_API_KEY'  # Replace with your API key
    city = 'London'
    url = f'http://api.openweathermap.org/data/2.5/weather?q={city}&appid={API_KEY}&units=metric'

    # Send the request and parse the response
    response = requests.get(url)
    if response.status_code == 200:
```

```
    data = response.json()
    city_name = data['name']
    temperature = data['main']['temp']
    description = data['weather'][0]['description']
    print(f"Weather in {city_name}: {temperature}°C, {description}")
else:
    print(f"Failed to retrieve data: {response.status_code}")


# Schedule the task to run every hour
schedule.every(1).hours.do(get_weather)


# Keep the script running and execute scheduled tasks
while True:
    schedule.run_pending()
    time.sleep(1)
```

## *Explanation of Automation:*

- The get_weather() function sends the request and processes the response.
- The schedule.every(1).hours.do(get_weather) line sets the function to run every hour.
- The while True loop keeps the script running and continuously checks for any pending tasks.

In this chapter, we introduced the concept of APIs and how Python can be used to interact with them for automation. We explored how to send data requests using Python's **requests** library, handle authentication using API keys, and automate tasks such as retrieving weather data.

Working with APIs is a fundamental part of automating interactions with external services and systems. By integrating APIs into your automation workflows, you can pull data from various sources, process it, and use it to make decisions or trigger other actions automatically.

In the next chapters, we will delve into more advanced automation tasks and explore how to integrate other services and tools to enhance your automation projects.

# Chapter 8: Web Scraping for Automation

## Using Python for Web Scraping and Automating Data Extraction

Web scraping is the process of extracting data from websites. It allows you to collect information that may not be readily available through traditional APIs, especially when dealing with unstructured data. Python provides powerful tools to scrape data and automate this process, making it an essential skill for automating data collection tasks.

In this chapter, we will cover how to use Python for web scraping, explore popular tools like **BeautifulSoup** and **Selenium**, and provide an example of automating the extraction of product prices from an e-commerce site.

### *What Is Web Scraping?*

Web scraping involves programmatically navigating a website and extracting relevant data. This is typically done by sending HTTP requests to the website, retrieving the HTML content, and parsing it to extract useful information. Web scraping can be applied in various scenarios such as:

- Extracting product details from e-commerce websites.

- Collecting news headlines or articles.
- Scraping job listings from employment websites.
- Gathering financial data from stock market sites.

**Web scraping is commonly used in:**

- **Market Research**: Automating the collection of competitor pricing, trends, and consumer sentiment.
- **Data Aggregation**: Collecting data from multiple sources and aggregating it for analysis.
- **Lead Generation**: Gathering contact information or business details from publicly available websites.

However, it's important to be aware of the **legal and ethical implications** of web scraping, such as respecting a website's terms of service, avoiding overloading the site with requests, and complying with data privacy regulations.

---

## Tools for Web Scraping

Python offers several libraries to facilitate web scraping, with **BeautifulSoup** and **Selenium** being the most commonly used tools.

### 1. BeautifulSoup

**BeautifulSoup** is a library used to parse HTML and XML documents, making it easy to navigate and search the DOM

(Document Object Model) structure. It is ideal for extracting specific elements from a static page.

- **How it works**: BeautifulSoup takes an HTML document and parses it into a tree of tags. You can then search through the tags to find specific elements, such as links, tables, or product prices.
- **Common tasks with BeautifulSoup**:
  - Navigating the DOM structure.
  - Extracting specific HTML elements, such as text, links, or images.
  - Filtering elements based on attributes or CSS classes.

**Installation**:

bash

```
pip install beautifulsoup4 requests
```

**Basic Example**:

python

```
import requests
from bs4 import BeautifulSoup

# Send a GET request to the website
url = 'https://example.com/products'
response = requests.get(url)
```

```
# Parse the HTML content
soup = BeautifulSoup(response.text, 'html.parser')

# Extract all product prices
prices = soup.find_all('span', class_='product-price')

# Print each price
for price in prices:
    print(price.text)
```

In this example, find_all is used to search for all span tags with a class of product-price. The result is a list of price elements that we can loop through and print.

## 2. Selenium

**Selenium** is a more powerful web scraping tool, primarily used for interacting with dynamic web pages that rely on JavaScript to load content. Unlike BeautifulSoup, which only works with static HTML, Selenium simulates a real web browser and allows you to control browser actions, such as clicking buttons, scrolling, and waiting for content to load.

- **How it works**: Selenium opens a browser (such as Chrome or Firefox), loads the page, and then interacts with the elements like a user would, allowing you to extract data from pages that require user interaction or JavaScript to render content.

- **Common tasks with Selenium**:

- o Automating browser actions (clicking buttons, filling forms).
- o Waiting for content to load (useful for JavaScript-heavy sites).
- o Scraping dynamic content that isn't available in the initial HTML response.

**Installation**:

bash

pip install selenium

You'll also need a web driver (such as **ChromeDriver** for Google Chrome) to control the browser. You can download ChromeDriver from here.

**Basic Example**:

python

```
from selenium import webdriver
from selenium.webdriver.common.by import By
import time

# Set up the browser driver
driver = webdriver.Chrome(executable_path='/path/to/chromedriver')

# Open the target URL
driver.get('https://example.com/products')
```

```
# Wait for the page to load (if necessary)
time.sleep(3)

# Extract product prices
prices = driver.find_elements(By.CLASS_NAME, 'product-price')

# Print each price
for price in prices:
    print(price.text)

# Close the browser
driver.quit()
```

In this example, we used Selenium to open a website, wait for the page to load, and extract the product prices based on their class names.

---

## Example: Automating the Extraction of Product Prices from an E-Commerce Site

Let's walk through an example where we automate the extraction of product prices from an e-commerce site using **BeautifulSoup** and **Selenium**. We'll demonstrate two approaches: one for static pages using BeautifulSoup and one for dynamic pages using Selenium.

### *Example 1: Using BeautifulSoup for Static Pages*

If the e-commerce website's product prices are embedded in the static HTML, we can use BeautifulSoup to extract them. Here's a simple script to extract product prices from a static e-commerce page:

python

```python
import requests
from bs4 import BeautifulSoup

# Define the e-commerce URL
url = 'https://www.example-ecommerce.com/products'

# Send a GET request
response = requests.get(url)

# Parse the HTML content using BeautifulSoup
soup = BeautifulSoup(response.text, 'html.parser')

# Find all product price elements
prices = soup.find_all('span', class_='price')  # Modify the class name based on the website's structure

# Print the extracted prices
for price in prices:
    print(price.text.strip())  # Strip any extra whitespace
```

In this case, we send a GET request to the website and parse the HTML to extract all the span elements with the class price. The extracted prices are then printed.

### *Example 2: Using Selenium for Dynamic Pages*

If the e-commerce site uses JavaScript to load the product prices (i.e., the prices are dynamically generated), BeautifulSoup alone won't work. We need to use Selenium to interact with the page and retrieve the data.

python

```python
from selenium import webdriver
from selenium.webdriver.common.by import By
import time

# Set up the Chrome browser driver
driver = webdriver.Chrome(executable_path='/path/to/chromedriver')

# Open the e-commerce site
driver.get('https://www.example-ecommerce.com/products')

# Wait for the page to load completely (adjust time as needed)
time.sleep(5)

# Extract product prices using Selenium
prices = driver.find_elements(By.CLASS_NAME, 'product-price')  # Modify the class name as needed

# Print the product prices
for price in prices:
    print(price.text)

# Close the browser
```

driver.quit()

In this example, Selenium is used to open the browser, wait for the page to load (since JavaScript is likely responsible for rendering the prices), and extract the prices using find_elements based on their class name.

---

In this chapter, we explored the powerful capabilities of **BeautifulSoup** and **Selenium** for web scraping and automating data extraction. BeautifulSoup is ideal for scraping static HTML pages, while Selenium is better suited for dealing with dynamic pages that rely on JavaScript for content rendering.

Web scraping is a valuable tool for automating data collection, enabling you to gather product prices, market trends, job listings, and more. By mastering web scraping techniques, you can automate the extraction of valuable data from a variety of sources, which can be integrated into larger automation workflows for analysis, decision-making, or reporting.

In the next chapters, we will continue exploring more advanced web scraping techniques, including handling pagination, dealing with CAPTCHA, and improving the efficiency of your scraping scripts.

# Chapter 9: Task Scheduling and Automation with Python

## Automating Recurring Tasks with Schedulers like Cron or Task Scheduler

Task scheduling is essential in automation, especially when you need to run scripts or tasks at specific times or intervals. Whether it's backing up files, sending emails, scraping websites, or generating reports, automating recurring tasks can save time and improve workflow efficiency. In this chapter, we will explore how to automate recurring tasks using scheduling tools like **Cron** (Linux/macOS) and **Task Scheduler** (Windows), and how to use Python to manage scheduled tasks.

### *What Is Task Scheduling?*

Task scheduling involves setting up a process that runs automatically at predefined times or intervals. This is particularly useful for routine tasks such as:

- Data backups
- Report generation
- Sending notifications or reminders
- Web scraping

- Periodic data processing

## Using Cron for Task Scheduling (Linux/macOS)

**Cron** is a time-based job scheduler in Unix-like operating systems (Linux and macOS). It allows you to schedule jobs (commands or scripts) to run at specified times or intervals. The cron daemon runs in the background and executes scheduled tasks based on the configuration in a file called a **crontab**.

### *1. Setting Up a Cron Job*

To schedule tasks using Cron, you need to edit the crontab file. You can do this by running the command:

bash

crontab -e

This opens the crontab file, where you can add new scheduled tasks. The syntax for a cron job entry is as follows:

bash

```
* * * * * /path/to/script.py
| | | | |
| | | | |
| | | | └── Day of the week (0 - 7) (0 and 7 are Sunday)
| | | └───── Month (1 - 12)
| | └──────── Day of the month (1 - 31)
| └─────────── Hour (0 - 23)
```

L————————— Minute (0 - 59)

For example, to run a Python script every day at 3:30 AM, add the following line:

bash

30 3 * * * /usr/bin/python3 /path/to/script.py

This line means:

- **30**: Run at minute 30
- **3**: Run at 3 AM
- **\***: Run every day of the month
- **\***: Run every month
- **\***: Run every day of the week

## 2. Checking Scheduled Cron Jobs

To check the current list of scheduled cron jobs, you can use:

bash

crontab -l

## 3. Stopping Cron Jobs

If you want to remove a cron job, you can edit the crontab again using crontab -e and delete the specific line. Alternatively, you can remove all cron jobs with:

bash

crontab -r

---

## Using Task Scheduler for Task Scheduling (Windows)

Windows provides the **Task Scheduler**, which is a built-in utility to schedule and automate tasks, such as running scripts or programs at specific times. Task Scheduler allows you to configure tasks with various triggers, such as daily, weekly, or at system startup.

### *1. Creating a Task in Task Scheduler*

To create a task using the Task Scheduler:

1. Open the Task Scheduler by searching for it in the Start menu.
2. In the **Action** pane, click **Create Basic Task**.
3. Follow the wizard to set up your task:
   - **Name the Task**: Provide a name for your task, such as "Run Python Script Daily."
   - **Set the Trigger**: Choose when to run the task (daily, weekly, on a specific event).
   - **Action**: Choose **Start a Program** and specify the path to the Python executable and the script you want to run. For example, if your Python script is script.py, set the program to:

bash

C:\Path\to\python.exe

Then add the script file as an argument:

bash

C:\Path\to\script.py

4. **Finish the Setup**: Set additional conditions or settings if necessary (e.g., run only when the computer is idle), and save the task.

## 2. Checking Scheduled Tasks

You can view and manage all tasks in Task Scheduler by selecting **Task Scheduler Library** from the left sidebar. It lists all active tasks and their triggers.

## 3. Editing or Deleting Scheduled Tasks

To edit or delete a task, simply right-click on it in Task Scheduler and choose the appropriate option.

---

## Scheduling Scripts to Run at Specific Times

Both **Cron** (for Linux/macOS) and **Task Scheduler** (for Windows) allow you to schedule scripts to run at specific times or intervals. You can also use Python to set up recurring tasks, for example, by automating email reports, file backups, or data scraping.

Let's look at an example of automating a daily email report generation using Python.

---

## Example: Automating Daily Email Reports

In this example, we will automate the process of sending a daily email report using Python. This can be applied to sending daily sales updates, system status reports, or any other data that needs to be emailed regularly.

### *Step 1: Install Required Libraries*

To send emails from Python, we need to use the smtplib library, which is included with Python. We will also use email.mime to structure the email content (subject, body, attachments).

bash

```
pip install smtplib email
```

### *Step 2: Create the Python Script*

Create a Python script (send_email_report.py) that generates the email and sends it.

python

```
import smtplib
from email.mime.multipart import MIMEMultipart
from email.mime.text import MIMEText
```

```python
from datetime import datetime

def send_report():
    # Email server details
    smtp_server = 'smtp.gmail.com'
    smtp_port = 587
    sender_email = 'your_email@gmail.com'
    receiver_email = 'recipient_email@example.com'
    password = 'your_email_password'  # Use environment variables for security in production

    # Create the email subject and body
    subject = f"Daily Report - {datetime.now().strftime('%Y-%m-%d')}"
    body = "This is your automated daily report."

    # Set up the email
    msg = MIMEMultipart()
    msg['From'] = sender_email
    msg['To'] = receiver_email
    msg['Subject'] = subject
    msg.attach(MIMEText(body, 'plain'))

    # Connect to the email server and send the email
    try:
        server = smtplib.SMTP(smtp_server, smtp_port)
        server.starttls()  # Secure the connection
        server.login(sender_email, password)
        server.sendmail(sender_email, receiver_email, msg.as_string())
        print("Email sent successfully!")
    except Exception as e:
```

```
    print(f"Error: {e}")
finally:
    server.quit()
```

```
# Run the function to send the email
send_report()
```

This script connects to Gmail's SMTP server, creates an email message, and sends it to a recipient. You can modify the body of the email to include dynamic content such as sales reports, performance statistics, or any other relevant information.

### Step 3: Schedule the Script to Run Daily

Now that we have the script to send the email, let's schedule it to run automatically every day. You can use **Cron** or **Task Scheduler** to automate this process, as described in earlier sections.

**For Linux/macOS (using Cron):**

Edit the crontab file by running crontab -e and add the following entry to run the script every day at 8:00 AM:

bash

```
0 8 * * * /usr/bin/python3 /path/to/send_email_report.py
```

**For Windows (using Task Scheduler):**

1. Open Task Scheduler and create a new task.
2. Set the trigger to **Daily** and set the time to 8:00 AM.

3. Set the action to **Start a Program** and specify the Python executable path and the path to your script.

---

In this chapter, we've explored how to automate recurring tasks using **Cron** (Linux/macOS) and **Task Scheduler** (Windows). By scheduling tasks such as sending daily email reports, scraping websites, or generating system backups, you can automate many time-consuming tasks.

We also demonstrated an example of automating the sending of daily email reports using Python, which can be extended to suit various use cases like performance tracking, automated alerts, or reporting.

Task scheduling is a powerful tool for automating repetitive tasks, and when combined with Python, it can streamline many aspects of your workflow, improving productivity and efficiency.

# Chapter 10: Introduction to Natural Language Processing (NLP)

## Basic NLP Concepts and Python Libraries (spaCy, NLTK)

Natural Language Processing (NLP) is a branch of artificial intelligence that focuses on the interaction between computers and human (natural) languages. It involves the development of algorithms and models that enable machines to process, understand, and generate human language in a way that is meaningful and useful. NLP applications are used in many areas such as chatbots, translation systems, sentiment analysis, and text summarization.

### 1. Core Concepts of NLP

Some fundamental concepts in NLP include:

- **Text Representation**: Converting text into numerical format so that machines can process it. Techniques like **bag of words**, **TF-IDF** (Term Frequency-Inverse Document Frequency), and **word embeddings** (e.g., Word2Vec) are commonly used for this purpose.

- **Tokenization**: Breaking text into smaller units, such as words, phrases, or sentences. This step is essential for many

NLP tasks because it helps to split the text into individual components for further analysis.

- **Part-of-Speech (POS) Tagging**: Identifying the grammatical role of each word in a sentence (e.g., noun, verb, adjective). This helps to understand the structure of the sentence.

- **Named Entity Recognition (NER)**: Identifying entities such as names of people, places, organizations, dates, etc., within a text.

- **Lemmatization and Stemming**: Reducing words to their base or root form. For example, "running" becomes "run," and "better" becomes "good" (lemmatization). Stemming is a simpler approach that removes suffixes to obtain a root word.

- **Sentiment Analysis**: Determining the sentiment expressed in a text, whether positive, negative, or neutral. This is useful for analyzing customer feedback, social media posts, and reviews.

## 2. Popular Python Libraries for NLP

There are two primary Python libraries that make it easy to perform NLP tasks: **spaCy** and **NLTK**.

- **spaCy**: spaCy is a fast and efficient NLP library designed for production use. It provides pre-trained models for various languages and supports tasks such as tokenization,

POS tagging, dependency parsing, NER, and word vectors. It is well-suited for large-scale text processing.

- **NLTK (Natural Language Toolkit)**: NLTK is one of the most widely used libraries in the Python ecosystem for NLP. It provides tools for text processing, tokenization, stemming, tagging, and more. NLTK is often used for educational purposes and research.

**Installation**:

bash

pip install spacy nltk

**Downloading spaCy's Pre-trained Model**:

bash

python -m spacy download en_core_web_sm

---

# Preprocessing and Tokenization

Data preprocessing is an essential step in NLP to prepare text for analysis. It includes tasks like removing noise (e.g., punctuation, stopwords), normalizing text, and tokenizing the text into words or sentences.

## *1. Preprocessing Text*

Common preprocessing steps in NLP include:

- **Lowercasing**: Converting all characters to lowercase to maintain uniformity.

- **Removing Punctuation**: Stripping punctuation marks, which are often irrelevant for text analysis.

- **Removing Stopwords**: Stopwords are common words like "the," "and," and "is," which do not carry significant meaning and can be removed to reduce noise.

- **Removing Special Characters**: Stripping non-alphabetic characters or symbols that do not add value to the analysis.

- **Lemmatization/Stemming**: Reducing words to their base forms to ensure that different variations of a word (e.g., "running," "ran") are treated as the same word.

## 2. Tokenization

Tokenization is the process of splitting text into smaller pieces, or tokens, such as words or sentences. This is often the first step in NLP tasks because it enables us to work with individual components of the text.

- **Word Tokenization**: Splitting text into words.
- **Sentence Tokenization**: Splitting text into sentences.

spaCy and NLTK both provide functions for tokenizing text:

**spaCy Example**:

python

```python
import spacy

# Load spaCy's pre-trained model
nlp = spacy.load("en_core_web_sm")

# Sample text
text = "Hello! How are you today? I hope you are doing well."

# Tokenize text
doc = nlp(text)
for token in doc:
    print(token.text)
```

## NLTK Example:

python

```python
import nltk
from nltk.tokenize import word_tokenize

# Sample text
text = "Hello! How are you today? I hope you are doing well."

# Tokenize text
tokens = word_tokenize(text)
print(tokens)
```

Both examples tokenize the text into words, and you can use the output for further NLP tasks like sentiment analysis, POS tagging, or named entity recognition.

# Example: Automating Text Analysis for Customer Feedback

In this example, we will automate the analysis of customer feedback using NLP techniques. We will use spaCy to preprocess and tokenize the text, and then perform sentiment analysis to determine whether the feedback is positive, negative, or neutral.

### Step 1: Install and Import Necessary Libraries
bash

```
pip install textblob
```

We will use the **TextBlob** library for sentiment analysis, which is simple to use and provides an easy way to get the polarity (positive/negative sentiment) of a text.

python

```
import spacy
from textblob import TextBlob

# Load spaCy model
nlp = spacy.load("en_core_web_sm")
```

### Step 2: Preprocess and Tokenize the Feedback
Let's assume we have a list of customer feedback, and we want to analyze each one.

python

```
# Sample customer feedback
feedback = [
    "The product is amazing! I'm really happy with the quality.",
    "Terrible service, I will never buy from here again.",
    "The delivery was on time, and the product is okay."
]

# Preprocess and tokenize feedback
for text in feedback:
    # Tokenize and preprocess text
    doc = nlp(text.lower())  # Convert text to lowercase
    tokens = [token.text for token in doc if not token.is_stop and not token.is_punct]
    print(f"Tokens: {tokens}")
```

In this step, we lowercase the text, remove stopwords and punctuation, and tokenize the feedback into words.

### *Step 3: Perform Sentiment Analysis*

Now, we will analyze the sentiment of each feedback text using **TextBlob**. TextBlob provides a polarity score where a positive score indicates positive sentiment, and a negative score indicates negative sentiment.

python

```
# Perform sentiment analysis on feedback
for text in feedback:
    # Analyze sentiment using TextBlob
```

```
blob = TextBlob(text)
sentiment = "Positive" if blob.sentiment.polarity > 0 else "Negative" if blob.sentiment.polarity < 0 else "Neutral"

print(f"Feedback: {text}\nSentiment: {sentiment}\n")
```

### *Step 4: Output*

The script will output the sentiment analysis results for each piece of feedback:

bash

```
Feedback: The product is amazing! I'm really happy with the quality.
Sentiment: Positive

Feedback: Terrible service, I will never buy from here again.
Sentiment: Negative

Feedback: The delivery was on time, and the product is okay.
Sentiment: Neutral
```

This example demonstrates how to automate the analysis of customer feedback by preprocessing the text, tokenizing it, and performing sentiment analysis. By automating this process, you can analyze large amounts of feedback in real-time, allowing you to make data-driven decisions to improve customer service, products, or marketing strategies.

In this chapter, we introduced the basics of **Natural Language Processing (NLP)** and explored some fundamental techniques like tokenization, preprocessing, and sentiment analysis. We discussed popular Python libraries for NLP, including **spaCy** and **NLTK**, and provided an example of automating the analysis of customer feedback using these tools.

NLP is a powerful tool for automating tasks related to text analysis, sentiment analysis, language translation, and more. By understanding and applying these techniques, you can streamline workflows, gain insights from large text datasets, and automate processes like customer feedback analysis.

As you progress, you can extend these concepts to more advanced NLP tasks such as text summarization, named entity recognition, and topic modeling. In the next chapters, we will explore more advanced NLP techniques and how they can be applied to real-world automation challenges.

# Chapter 11: Building Simple AI Models with Python

---

## Introduction to Building AI Models Using Scikit-learn

Scikit-learn is one of the most widely used libraries for building machine learning models in Python. It provides simple and efficient tools for data mining and data analysis, built on top of NumPy, SciPy, and matplotlib. Scikit-learn simplifies the process of building AI models by providing easy-to-use APIs for various machine learning tasks, such as regression, classification, and clustering.

In this chapter, we will introduce how to build simple AI models using Scikit-learn, focusing on key machine learning tasks such as regression, classification, and clustering. We will also walk through a real-world example of predicting customer churn using a machine learning model.

### *Key Concepts in AI Modeling*

1. **Machine Learning Models**: Machine learning algorithms can be used to create predictive models based on input data. These models can be classified into three primary categories:
   - **Regression**: Predicting continuous values (e.g., predicting house prices, stock prices).

- ○ **Classification**: Predicting discrete classes or categories (e.g., spam detection, disease diagnosis).
- ○ **Clustering**: Grouping similar data points into clusters (e.g., customer segmentation, market basket analysis).

2. **Training a Model**: In machine learning, you train a model using labeled data. The model learns patterns from this data, which it then uses to make predictions or classifications on new, unseen data.

3. **Evaluating a Model**: After training a model, it is important to evaluate its performance using appropriate metrics such as accuracy, precision, recall, F1 score for classification tasks, or mean squared error (MSE) for regression tasks.

---

## Regression, Classification, and Clustering

### *1. Regression*

Regression algorithms are used for predicting continuous numeric values. They are suitable for tasks where the goal is to predict a quantity, such as house prices, stock prices, or temperature.

- **Linear Regression**: One of the simplest and most commonly used regression models. It finds the relationship between input features and the target variable by fitting a straight line to the data.

- **Ridge and Lasso Regression**: Variants of linear regression that add regularization to reduce overfitting.

## 2. Classification

Classification algorithms are used when the target variable is categorical. The model learns to classify input data into predefined classes or labels.

- **Logistic Regression**: Despite its name, it is a classification algorithm. It is used for binary classification (e.g., spam or not spam).
- **Support Vector Machines (SVM)**: A powerful classifier that works by finding the hyperplane that best separates the data into classes.
- **Random Forest**: An ensemble learning method that creates a collection of decision trees and combines their results for classification.

## 3. Clustering

Clustering is an unsupervised learning technique used to group similar data points. Unlike regression and classification, clustering algorithms don't require labeled data.

- **K-Means Clustering**: A widely used clustering algorithm that partitions data into k clusters based on their feature similarity.
- **Hierarchical Clustering**: Builds a tree of clusters by iteratively merging smaller clusters.

---

## Example: Predicting Customer Churn with Python

In this example, we will build a machine learning model to predict **customer churn**. Customer churn refers to the phenomenon where customers stop using a service. A churn prediction model helps businesses understand the likelihood of customer attrition, allowing them to take proactive measures to retain customers.

For this, we will use a classification algorithm, specifically **Logistic Regression**, to predict whether a customer will churn (1) or not churn (0) based on various features like age, account type, and usage data.

### *Step 1: Install Required Libraries*

First, we need to install the required libraries for data manipulation and machine learning:

bash

```
pip install pandas scikit-learn
```

### *Step 2: Load and Prepare the Data*

Let's assume we have a dataset customer_churn.csv containing customer data with features such as age, account type, and usage, along with a target variable churn (1 if the customer churned, 0 if not). We will use pandas to load and preprocess the data.

python

```python
import pandas as pd
from sklearn.model_selection import train_test_split
from sklearn.linear_model import LogisticRegression
from sklearn.metrics import accuracy_score, confusion_matrix
from sklearn.preprocessing import StandardScaler

# Load the dataset
data = pd.read_csv('customer_churn.csv')

# Display the first few rows of the data
print(data.head())
```

Sample data might look like this:

plaintext

```
| Age | Account_Type | Usage | Churn |
|-----|--------------|-------|-------|
| 25  | Basic        | 100   | 0     |
| 40  | Premium      | 500   | 1     |
| 35  | Basic        | 200   | 0     |
| 50  | Premium      | 800   | 1     |
```

### *Step 3: Preprocess the Data*

Before we train the model, we need to preprocess the data. This includes handling any missing values, encoding categorical variables, and scaling the data.

python

```python
# Handle missing values (if any)
data.fillna(method='ffill', inplace=True)

# Encode categorical data (Account_Type) using one-hot encoding
data = pd.get_dummies(data, columns=['Account_Type'], drop_first=True)

# Split the data into features (X) and target (y)
X = data.drop('Churn', axis=1)  # Features
y = data['Churn']  # Target

# Split the data into training and testing sets
X_train, X_test, y_train, y_test = train_test_split(X, y, test_size=0.3, random_state=42)

# Scale the features to improve model performance
scaler = StandardScaler()
X_train = scaler.fit_transform(X_train)
X_test = scaler.transform(X_test)
```

### *Step 4: Train the Logistic Regression Model*

Now, we'll train a Logistic Regression model on the training data.

python

```python
# Initialize the logistic regression model
model = LogisticRegression()

# Train the model on the training data
model.fit(X_train, y_train)
```

### Step 5: Make Predictions

After training the model, we can use it to make predictions on the test data.

python

```python
# Make predictions on the test data
y_pred = model.predict(X_test)

# Print the accuracy of the model
accuracy = accuracy_score(y_test, y_pred)
print(f"Accuracy: {accuracy * 100:.2f}%")
```

### Step 6: Evaluate the Model

To evaluate the model, we can look at additional metrics such as the confusion matrix, which shows the number of correct and incorrect predictions.

python

```python
# Generate the confusion matrix
cm = confusion_matrix(y_test, y_pred)
print("Confusion Matrix:")
```

print(cm)

The confusion matrix will help us understand how well the model is distinguishing between customers who churned and those who did not. The matrix contains four values:

- **True Positives (TP)**: Correctly predicted churned customers.
- **True Negatives (TN)**: Correctly predicted non-churned customers.
- **False Positives (FP)**: Incorrectly predicted non-churned customers as churned.
- **False Negatives (FN)**: Incorrectly predicted churned customers as non-churned.

### *Step 7: Output the Results*

The final output might look like this:

plaintext

Accuracy: 85.00%
Confusion Matrix:
[[50  5]
 [10 35]]

This indicates that the model correctly predicted 50 customers as non-churned and 35 customers as churned. The accuracy score shows how often the model was correct.

In this chapter, we introduced the process of building simple AI models with Python using **Scikit-learn**. We covered the three main types of machine learning tasks: regression, classification, and clustering. We also walked through a real-world example of predicting **customer churn** using **Logistic Regression**, one of the most commonly used classification algorithms.

Key steps in building an AI model include:

- **Data preparation**: Cleaning, encoding, and scaling the data.
- **Model selection**: Choosing the right algorithm (e.g., logistic regression for classification).
- **Model training**: Using the training data to build the model.
- **Model evaluation**: Measuring the model's performance using metrics like accuracy and confusion matrix.

By following these steps, you can create AI models to automate tasks like customer churn prediction, sales forecasting, or sentiment analysis. As you progress, you can experiment with more complex models and techniques to improve your predictions and automate even more sophisticated tasks.

# Chapter 12: Automating Machine Learning Workflows

---

## End-to-End Automation of ML Workflows

Machine learning (ML) workflows typically involve several stages, including data collection, data preprocessing, model training, model evaluation, and deployment. Automating these stages is crucial to ensure reproducibility, efficiency, and scalability. By automating the entire process, you can run experiments, tune models, track results, and deploy models with minimal human intervention.

In this chapter, we will discuss how to automate the entire ML pipeline using tools like **MLflow** and **TensorFlow**. We will also explore an example of automating the training and testing of an ML model for a classification task.

### 1. What Is an End-to-End ML Workflow?

An end-to-end ML workflow involves the following steps:

1. **Data Collection**: Collecting raw data from various sources (databases, APIs, files, etc.).

2. **Data Preprocessing**: Cleaning, transforming, and preparing data for model training (e.g., handling missing values, scaling, encoding).

3. **Model Training**: Using the preprocessed data to train a machine learning model (e.g., classification, regression).

4. **Model Evaluation**: Assessing the model's performance using metrics like accuracy, precision, recall, or mean squared error.

5. **Model Tuning**: Fine-tuning the model to improve its performance (e.g., hyperparameter optimization).

6. **Model Deployment**: Deploying the trained model to production for real-time predictions or batch processing.

Automating this workflow ensures that the process is repeatable, consistent, and efficient. It allows for faster iteration and can be integrated into production systems to make predictions automatically.

---

## Using Libraries Like MLflow and TensorFlow

### 1. MLflow: Managing the ML Lifecycle

**MLflow** is an open-source platform for managing the end-to-end machine learning lifecycle. It helps track experiments, manage models, and organize workflows. MLflow consists of several components:

- **MLflow Tracking**: Used for logging and tracking experiments, including parameters, metrics, and artifacts.

- **MLflow Projects**: A way to package code, data, and dependencies into reusable and reproducible units.
- **MLflow Models**: A system for managing and serving machine learning models in various formats.
- **MLflow Registry**: A central repository for managing models in a collaborative environment.

MLflow allows you to automate tasks like experiment tracking, model versioning, and model deployment, making it an essential tool for managing machine learning workflows.

## 2. TensorFlow: Streamlining Model Development

**TensorFlow** is an open-source machine learning library primarily used for deep learning tasks. It provides flexible tools for building, training, and deploying models, and integrates well with other libraries to automate various stages of the ML workflow.

- **TensorFlow Keras**: High-level API for building and training deep learning models in TensorFlow.
- **TensorFlow Extended (TFX)**: A platform for deploying production ML pipelines, including model training, evaluation, and deployment.
- **TensorFlow Serving**: A system for deploying models in production environments.

TensorFlow makes it easy to automate model training, hyperparameter tuning, and deployment, especially for deep learning applications.

---

## Example: Automating the Training and Testing of a Model

Let's walk through an example of automating the training and testing of a machine learning model using **MLflow** and **TensorFlow**. In this example, we will build and automate the training of a deep learning model to classify images from the **Fashion MNIST** dataset, which contains grayscale images of clothing items.

### Step 1: Install Required Libraries

First, we need to install MLflow and TensorFlow.

bash

```
pip install mlflow tensorflow
```

### Step 2: Load the Dataset and Preprocess the Data

The Fashion MNIST dataset is available in TensorFlow and can be easily loaded using Keras.

python

```
import tensorflow as tf
import mlflow
import mlflow.keras
```

```
from tensorflow.keras import layers, models
from sklearn.model_selection import train_test_split

# Load the Fashion MNIST dataset
(x_train, y_train), (x_test, y_test) = tf.keras.datasets.fashion_mnist.load_data()

# Normalize pixel values to be between 0 and 1
x_train, x_test = x_train / 255.0, x_test / 255.0

# Reshape the data to fit the input shape of the model (28x28x1)
x_train = x_train.reshape(-1, 28, 28, 1)
x_test = x_test.reshape(-1, 28, 28, 1)
```

### Step 3: Build and Train the Model

Next, we define a simple convolutional neural network (CNN) model using Keras. We will then automate the training process using MLflow's tracking capabilities.

python

```python
# Define the CNN model
model = models.Sequential([
    layers.Conv2D(32, (3, 3), activation='relu', input_shape=(28, 28, 1)),
    layers.MaxPooling2D((2, 2)),
    layers.Conv2D(64, (3, 3), activation='relu'),
    layers.MaxPooling2D((2, 2)),
    layers.Conv2D(64, (3, 3), activation='relu'),
    layers.Flatten(),
    layers.Dense(64, activation='relu'),
    layers.Dense(10, activation='softmax')
```

```python
])

# Compile the model
model.compile(optimizer='adam',
              loss='sparse_categorical_crossentropy',
              metrics=['accuracy'])

# Log the experiment with MLflow
with mlflow.start_run():
    # Log hyperparameters
    mlflow.log_param("batch_size", 64)
    mlflow.log_param("epochs", 10)

    # Train the model
    model.fit(x_train, y_train, epochs=10, batch_size=64, validation_data=(x_test,
y_test))

    # Log the model
    mlflow.keras.log_model(model, "fashion_mnist_model")

    # Evaluate the model
    test_loss, test_acc = model.evaluate(x_test, y_test)
    mlflow.log_metric("test_accuracy", test_acc)

    print(f"Test accuracy: {test_acc}")
```

## *Explanation of the Code:*

- **Loading the Dataset**: The Fashion MNIST dataset is loaded and normalized to fit the range required by the model.

- **Model Definition**: A simple CNN is defined with three convolutional layers, followed by a dense layer and an output layer.
- **Training**: The model is trained using the fit() function, and the experiment is tracked using **MLflow**.
  - ○ **Hyperparameters**: Batch size and number of epochs are logged as parameters.
  - ○ **Model**: The trained model is logged in MLflow for later use.
  - ○ **Metrics**: The model's accuracy on the test set is logged as a metric.

***Step 4: Automating Model Testing and Hyperparameter Tuning***

Once the model is trained, we can use MLflow to automate the testing and hyperparameter tuning process. Let's demonstrate hyperparameter tuning using MLflow's **Grid Search** feature (or manually adjusting hyperparameters).

python

```python
# Log different hyperparameters
for batch_size in [32, 64]:
    for epochs in [5, 10]:
        with mlflow.start_run():
            mlflow.log_param("batch_size", batch_size)
            mlflow.log_param("epochs", epochs)

            # Train the model with different hyperparameters
```

```
model.fit(x_train, y_train, epochs=epochs, batch_size=batch_size,
validation_data=(x_test, y_test))

# Log the model
mlflow.keras.log_model(model,
f"fashion_mnist_model_{batch_size}_{epochs}")

# Evaluate and log the metrics
test_loss, test_acc = model.evaluate(x_test, y_test)
mlflow.log_metric("test_accuracy", test_acc)
print(f"Test accuracy for batch_size={batch_size}, epochs={epochs}:
{test_acc}")
```

## Step 5: Retrieving and Using the Best Model

Once the model is trained and evaluated, you can retrieve the best-performing model from MLflow for future use or deployment.

python

```
# Load the best model (example)
best_model                                                =
mlflow.keras.load_model('models:/fashion_mnist_model/Production')
```

---

In this chapter, we demonstrated how to automate the machine learning workflow using **MLflow** and **TensorFlow**. We covered the steps for:

- **Loading and preprocessing data**: Normalizing and reshaping data for input to the model.
- **Building and training the model**: Using a simple CNN for classifying images from the Fashion MNIST dataset.
- **Tracking experiments**: Using MLflow to log hyperparameters, metrics, and models during training.
- **Automating hyperparameter tuning**: Running multiple experiments with different configurations.

By automating the machine learning workflow, you can quickly iterate on different models, tune hyperparameters, and track experiments in a reproducible way. MLflow not only helps manage models and track experiments but also ensures that the entire machine learning lifecycle, from training to deployment, is automated and streamlined.

This workflow is scalable to more complex models and larger datasets, and can be extended for tasks such as deep learning, reinforcement learning, and more advanced hyperparameter optimization techniques. As you build more sophisticated models, automating the workflow will become an essential practice for maintaining efficiency and consistency in your AI projects.

# Chapter 13: Introduction to Deep Learning for Automation

## Understanding Neural Networks and Deep Learning

Deep learning is a subset of machine learning that focuses on using neural networks with many layers to model complex patterns in data. It has been a transformative technology in fields like computer vision, natural language processing, and speech recognition. Deep learning algorithms are designed to learn from vast amounts of data and improve their performance over time.

### 1. What Is a Neural Network?

A neural network is a computational model inspired by the way the human brain works. It consists of layers of interconnected nodes (neurons), which work together to solve problems like classification, regression, and clustering.

- **Neurons**: Each node or neuron in a neural network receives one or more inputs, processes them using an activation function, and passes the result to the next layer.
- **Layers**:
    - **Input Layer**: The first layer that receives the raw data (e.g., image pixels or text).

o **Hidden Layers**: Layers between the input and output layers where the actual computations occur. These layers help the model learn complex representations of the data.

o **Output Layer**: The final layer that provides the model's prediction, such as a classification label or a regression value.

## *2. How Deep Learning Works*

In deep learning, the term "deep" refers to the number of hidden layers in a neural network. A deep neural network can have many hidden layers, allowing it to learn more abstract and complex patterns in data. These networks are trained using algorithms like **backpropagation**, which adjusts the weights of the connections between neurons based on the error between the predicted output and the true output.

## *3. Key Components of Deep Learning*

- **Activation Functions**: Functions like **ReLU (Rectified Linear Unit)**, **sigmoid**, and **tanh** that introduce non-linearity to the network, enabling it to learn complex patterns.
- **Loss Function**: A function used to measure how well the model's predictions align with the true labels. For classification, common loss functions include **categorical crossentropy** and **binary crossentropy**.

- **Optimizer**: Algorithms like **Stochastic Gradient Descent (SGD)**, **Adam**, and **RMSprop** are used to adjust the weights of the neurons based on the loss function.

## 4. Advantages of Deep Learning

- **High Accuracy**: Deep learning models are highly accurate, especially in tasks such as image recognition, speech recognition, and natural language processing.
- **Feature Learning**: Deep learning models can automatically learn relevant features from raw data, such as raw images or text, reducing the need for manual feature engineering.
- **Scalability**: Deep learning models can handle large datasets and can scale with more data, improving performance over time.

---

## Libraries for Deep Learning: TensorFlow and Keras

Deep learning frameworks provide the tools necessary to build, train, and deploy deep neural networks. The two most widely used libraries for deep learning are **TensorFlow** and **Keras**.

### 1. TensorFlow

**TensorFlow** is an open-source deep learning framework developed by Google. It provides a comprehensive ecosystem of tools for building and deploying machine learning models, especially for deep learning.

- **Flexible**: TensorFlow supports both low-level and high-level APIs, making it suitable for beginners and experts.
- **Scalable**: It can run on a single machine or across multiple machines, making it ideal for large-scale deep learning tasks.
- **TensorFlow Hub**: A library of reusable pre-trained models for tasks like image classification, text analysis, and object detection.

## 2. Keras

**Keras** is a high-level deep learning API that runs on top of TensorFlow (and other backends like Theano and Microsoft Cognitive Toolkit). It provides an easy-to-use interface for building and training neural networks.

- **User-Friendly**: Keras is designed to be easy to use and highly modular, making it simple to build and experiment with deep learning models.
- **Integration with TensorFlow**: As of TensorFlow 2.0, Keras is integrated directly into TensorFlow, providing a seamless experience for building and deploying models.

**Keras Example**: Keras allows you to quickly define and train deep learning models in just a few lines of code. Here's an example of building a simple feed-forward neural network for image classification.

---

## Example: Automating Image Recognition Tasks with Deep Learning

In this example, we will automate the process of training and testing a deep learning model for image recognition. We will use the **Fashion MNIST** dataset, which consists of grayscale images of 10 clothing categories (e.g., T-shirts, pants, shoes, etc.).

We will use **Keras** (with TensorFlow as the backend) to build and train a convolutional neural network (CNN), a type of deep learning model that is highly effective for image classification tasks.

### Step 1: Install TensorFlow

First, install TensorFlow and Keras:

bash

```
pip install tensorflow
```

### Step 2: Load and Preprocess the Data

We will load the Fashion MNIST dataset, normalize the image data, and split it into training and testing sets.

python

```
import tensorflow as tf
from tensorflow.keras import layers, models
from tensorflow.keras.datasets import fashion_mnist

# Load the Fashion MNIST dataset
(x_train, y_train), (x_test, y_test) = fashion_mnist.load_data()

# Normalize the image data to be between 0 and 1
x_train, x_test = x_train / 255.0, x_test / 255.0

# Reshape the data to fit the input shape of the model (28x28x1)
x_train = x_train.reshape(-1, 28, 28, 1)
x_test = x_test.reshape(-1, 28, 28, 1)
```

### *Step 3: Build the CNN Model*

We will define a simple CNN for image classification. The model will consist of convolutional layers, pooling layers, and a dense output layer.

python

```
# Define the CNN model
model = models.Sequential([
    layers.Conv2D(32, (3, 3), activation='relu', input_shape=(28, 28, 1)),
    layers.MaxPooling2D((2, 2)),
    layers.Conv2D(64, (3, 3), activation='relu'),
    layers.MaxPooling2D((2, 2)),
    layers.Conv2D(64, (3, 3), activation='relu'),
    layers.Flatten(),
    layers.Dense(64, activation='relu'),
```

```
    layers.Dense(10, activation='softmax')
])
```

```
# Compile the model
model.compile(optimizer='adam',
          loss='sparse_categorical_crossentropy',
          metrics=['accuracy'])
```

### Step 4: Train the Model

Now we will train the model using the training data.

python

```
# Train the model on the training data
model.fit(x_train, y_train, epochs=5)
```

### Step 5: Evaluate the Model

After training the model, we will evaluate its performance using the test data.

python

```
# Evaluate the model on the test data
test_loss, test_acc = model.evaluate(x_test, y_test)
print(f"Test accuracy: {test_acc}")
```

### Step 6: Automate the Model Training and Testing

You can automate the entire process of training and testing by placing the training script inside a function and scheduling it to run at specific intervals. For example, you could use **Cron**

(Linux/macOS) or **Task Scheduler** (Windows) to schedule the script to run daily, retraining the model with the latest data.

Alternatively, you can integrate the model training into a larger pipeline using tools like **MLflow** or **TensorFlow Extended (TFX)** to track experiments and automate model retraining, hyperparameter tuning, and deployment.

---

In this chapter, we introduced the basics of **deep learning** and how to build deep learning models using **TensorFlow** and **Keras**. We covered key concepts such as neural networks, layers, and activation functions, and demonstrated how to automate image recognition tasks using deep learning.

We also explored the power of deep learning for automating tasks like image recognition and classification. With the help of TensorFlow and Keras, we were able to build a convolutional neural network (CNN) for recognizing clothing items from the Fashion MNIST dataset. The automated training and testing process can be extended to other use cases such as object detection, facial recognition, and autonomous systems.

As you continue exploring deep learning, you can scale this approach to more complex datasets and tasks, building models that automate even more advanced applications in computer vision, natural language processing, and beyond.

# Chapter 14: Computer Vision for Automation

## Using Python for Image Processing and Automation

Computer Vision is a subfield of Artificial Intelligence (AI) that focuses on enabling computers to interpret and make decisions based on visual data, such as images and videos. With the help of various libraries, Python makes it easy to perform tasks like image classification, object detection, facial recognition, and more.

In this chapter, we will explore how to use Python for image processing and automation. We will cover how to leverage powerful libraries like **OpenCV** and **Pillow (PIL)** to automate computer vision tasks and provide a practical example of automating object detection in video feeds.

## Libraries for Computer Vision in Python

There are several popular Python libraries for computer vision tasks. The two most widely used libraries are **OpenCV** and **Pillow (PIL)**.

### 1. OpenCV (Open Source Computer Vision Library)

**OpenCV** is an open-source library that provides tools for real-time computer vision tasks. It supports a wide variety of operations such as reading, writing, and processing images and videos, performing feature detection, and applying image filters.

**Key features of OpenCV:**

- Image and video reading/writing.
- Geometric transformations (e.g., resizing, rotating, cropping).
- Object detection (e.g., face, eye detection).
- Image filtering (e.g., smoothing, sharpening).
- Feature detection and tracking (e.g., edge detection, keypoint matching).

**Installation**:

bash

pip install opencv-python

## 2. Pillow (PIL)

**Pillow** (PIL) is a powerful library for opening, manipulating, and saving many different image file formats. While OpenCV is more geared toward real-time video and image processing, Pillow is often used for simpler tasks like image loading, editing, and saving.

**Key features of Pillow:**

- Opening, resizing, cropping, and saving images.
- Image enhancement (e.g., brightness, contrast).
- Image filtering and transformations.
- Drawing text, lines, and shapes on images.

**Installation**:

bash

pip install pillow

---

## Image Processing for Automation

Image processing is a key aspect of computer vision, where raw image data is transformed to improve its quality or extract useful features. These tasks can be automated to streamline workflows in fields like security, manufacturing, healthcare, and entertainment.

Some common image processing tasks include:

- **Grayscale Conversion**: Converting a color image to grayscale to reduce the complexity of processing.
- **Resizing**: Scaling images to a specific resolution.
- **Blurring**: Smoothing images to remove noise.
- **Edge Detection**: Identifying edges in an image to highlight object boundaries.

- **Thresholding**: Converting an image to binary format (black and white) based on pixel intensity.

Here's an example of basic image processing using OpenCV and Pillow:

**OpenCV Example**:

python

```
import cv2

# Load an image
image = cv2.imread('image.jpg')

# Convert to grayscale
gray_image = cv2.cvtColor(image, cv2.COLOR_BGR2GRAY)

# Resize the image
resized_image = cv2.resize(image, (200, 200))

# Save the processed image
cv2.imwrite('gray_image.jpg', gray_image)
cv2.imwrite('resized_image.jpg', resized_image)
```

**Pillow Example**:

python

```
from PIL import Image, ImageEnhance
```

```
# Open an image
image = Image.open('image.jpg')

# Convert to grayscale
gray_image = image.convert('L')

# Resize the image
resized_image = image.resize((200, 200))

# Enhance brightness
enhancer = ImageEnhance.Brightness(image)
bright_image = enhancer.enhance(1.5)

# Save the processed images
gray_image.save('gray_image_pil.jpg')
resized_image.save('resized_image_pil.jpg')
bright_image.save('bright_image_pil.jpg')
```

---

## Example: Automating Object Detection in Video Feeds

In this section, we will automate object detection in video feeds using **OpenCV**. Specifically, we will use a pre-trained object detection model to identify and track objects in real-time from a video stream.

We will use a **Haar Cascade Classifier**, a popular machine learning-based approach for detecting objects, including faces, eyes, or even vehicles, in an image or video stream.

143

### *Step 1: Install Dependencies*

First, make sure you have **OpenCV** installed:

bash

```
pip install opencv-python
```

### *Step 2: Load the Pre-trained Model*

OpenCV provides several pre-trained models for object detection, including models for face detection. We will use one of the pre-trained Haar Cascade classifiers for face detection.

Download the **Haar Cascade Classifier** for face detection from the OpenCV repository: Haar Cascade Classifier for Face Detection

Ensure that the haarcascade_frontalface_default.xml file is accessible in your project directory.

### *Step 3: Set Up Video Feed and Object Detection*

Now, let's write the code to capture a video feed from your webcam, perform object detection, and display the results.

python

```
import cv2

# Load the pre-trained Haar Cascade classifier for face detection
face_cascade = cv2.CascadeClassifier('haarcascade_frontalface_default.xml')

# Open a video capture object (0 for webcam, or provide a file path for video)
```

```
cap = cv2.VideoCapture(0)

while True:
    # Read a frame from the video feed
    ret, frame = cap.read()

    # Convert the frame to grayscale for better performance
    gray = cv2.cvtColor(frame, cv2.COLOR_BGR2GRAY)

    # Detect faces in the grayscale image
    faces      =       face_cascade.detectMultiScale(gray,       scaleFactor=1.1,
minNeighbors=5, minSize=(30, 30))

    # Draw rectangles around the faces detected
    for (x, y, w, h) in faces:
        cv2.rectangle(frame, (x, y), (x + w, y + h), (255, 0, 0), 2)

    # Display the frame with detections
    cv2.imshow('Video Feed', frame)

    # Exit the loop if the user presses 'q'
    if cv2.waitKey(1) & 0xFF == ord('q'):
        break

# Release the video capture object and close any open windows
cap.release()
cv2.destroyAllWindows()
```

## *Explanation of the Code:*

1. **Haar Cascade Classifier**: We load the Haar Cascade Classifier for face detection using cv2.CascadeClassifier().

2. **Video Capture**: cv2.VideoCapture(0) captures video from your default webcam (you can replace 0 with a video file path to process pre-recorded videos).

3. **Face Detection**: face_cascade.detectMultiScale() detects objects (faces in this case) in the image.

4. **Drawing Rectangles**: cv2.rectangle() draws a rectangle around each detected face.

5. **Display the Video Feed**: cv2.imshow() displays the video feed with object detection in real-time.

6. **Exit the Loop**: The loop continues until you press 'q' to quit.

### *Step 4: Automating Object Detection in Video Feeds*

By running this script, the program automatically processes the video feed and detects faces in real time. The rectangles drawn around detected faces demonstrate how object detection can be automated in video feeds. This can be extended to detect other objects like cars, pedestrians, or even specific features (e.g., eyes, smiles) depending on the chosen classifier.

---

In this chapter, we explored how to use Python for image processing and automation with libraries like **OpenCV** and **Pillow**. We covered essential image processing tasks like resizing, blurring, and edge detection, which are often the first steps in automating computer vision tasks.

We also demonstrated how to automate object detection in video feeds using **OpenCV**'s pre-trained Haar Cascade Classifier. The example of detecting faces in real-time from a webcam feed shows how computer vision can be applied to live video streams for automation tasks such as security, surveillance, and monitoring.

With tools like OpenCV and Pillow, you can automate a wide range of computer vision tasks in industries like healthcare, retail, manufacturing, and entertainment. The potential applications for computer vision automation are vast, from self-driving cars to automated quality inspection systems.

As you progress, you can explore more advanced topics like deep learning-based object detection (e.g., using models like YOLO or SSD), facial recognition, and optical character recognition (OCR).

# Chapter 15: Voice Recognition and Automation with Python

---

## Integrating Speech Recognition into Automation Tasks

Voice recognition technology allows computers to interpret and respond to spoken language. It has found applications in voice assistants like Alexa, Siri, and Google Assistant, as well as in systems for automating tasks using voice commands.

In this chapter, we will explore how to integrate **speech recognition** into automation tasks using Python. We will leverage libraries like **SpeechRecognition** and **PyAudio** to process and recognize spoken commands. This chapter also includes an example of automating voice commands for smart home devices, where users can control devices like lights, thermostats, and more using their voice.

---

## Libraries for Speech Recognition in Python

There are several libraries available in Python for speech recognition, with **SpeechRecognition** and **PyAudio** being the most widely used.

## *1. SpeechRecognition*

The **SpeechRecognition** library provides a simple interface for converting speech into text. It supports multiple speech recognition engines, including Google's Web Speech API, Microsoft Bing Voice Recognition, and more. The library also allows you to work with audio files and perform speech-to-text conversion locally or remotely.

**Key features of SpeechRecognition:**

- Converts speech into text from both microphones and audio files.
- Supports various recognition engines and APIs.
- Works with real-time or pre-recorded audio.

**Installation:**

bash

pip install SpeechRecognition

## *2. PyAudio*

**PyAudio** is a library used to work with audio data, enabling real-time audio capture and playback. It is required to interface with a microphone for capturing speech in real-time.

**Key features of PyAudio:**

- Allows access to microphone input and speaker output.

- Facilitates audio recording, playback, and processing.
- Works well with SpeechRecognition to capture live speech.

**Installation**:

bash

pip install pyaudio

*Note*: On some systems, you may need additional dependencies to install PyAudio. If you face issues installing PyAudio, consider following platform-specific installation instructions or use an alternative like **sounddevice**.

---

## Example: Automating Voice Commands for Smart Home Devices

In this example, we will use Python to automate voice commands for controlling a smart home device, such as turning a light on or off, adjusting a thermostat, or controlling other smart devices. We will leverage the **SpeechRecognition** library for recognizing voice commands and integrate them into an automation system.

### *Step 1: Set Up the Environment*

First, ensure you have the necessary libraries installed:

bash

```
pip install SpeechRecognition pyaudio
```

Next, you can simulate controlling a smart home device. For the sake of simplicity, we will print commands like "Turning light on" or "Adjusting thermostat" based on recognized voice commands.

### Step 2: Capture and Recognize Speech

We will use the **SpeechRecognition** library to capture speech from the microphone and recognize the spoken command. Then, based on the recognized command, we will automate the corresponding task.

```python
import speech_recognition as sr

# Initialize recognizer
recognizer = sr.Recognizer()

# Function to recognize speech and automate tasks
def recognize_voice_command():
    with sr.Microphone() as source:
        print("Say something...")
        recognizer.adjust_for_ambient_noise(source)  # Adjust for ambient noise
        audio = recognizer.listen(source)  # Listen to the microphone

        try:
            # Recognize speech using Google's speech recognition engine
            command = recognizer.recognize_google(audio)
            print(f"Recognized command: {command}")
            return command.lower()
        except sr.UnknownValueError:
```

```
        print("Sorry, I did not understand that.")
    except sr.RequestError:
        print("Sorry, the speech recognition service is unavailable.")
    return None


# Function to automate tasks based on voice commands
def automate_task(command):
    if 'light on' in command:
        print("Turning light on...")
    elif 'light off' in command:
        print("Turning light off...")
    elif 'thermostat up' in command:
        print("Increasing thermostat temperature...")
    elif 'thermostat down' in command:
        print("Decreasing thermostat temperature...")
    else:
        print("Command not recognized. Please try again.")


# Main loop to continuously listen for commands
while True:
    command = recognize_voice_command()
    if command:
        automate_task(command)
    else:
        print("Waiting for a new command...")
```

## *Explanation of the Code:*

1. **Speech Capture**: The program uses the Microphone class from the **SpeechRecognition** library to capture audio from

the microphone. The recognizer.listen() function listens to the microphone for speech input.

2. **Speech Recognition**: The captured audio is then passed to Google's speech recognition engine via recognizer.recognize_google(audio), which converts the speech to text.

3. **Voice Command Processing**: The recognized text is matched against predefined commands (e.g., "light on," "thermostat up"). If a match is found, the corresponding action (e.g., "Turning light on") is performed.

4. **Automation Logic**: Based on the recognized command, the automate_task() function performs the relevant task, like turning the light on/off or adjusting the thermostat. In this case, we simulate the actions by printing messages to the console.

5. **Continuous Listening**: The script continuously listens for commands in a loop, allowing for real-time automation of voice commands.

### *Step 3: Test and Run the Script*

Run the script, and speak the commands into the microphone. Some example voice commands you can try include:

- "Turn light on"
- "Turn light off"
- "Thermostat up"

- "Thermostat down"

The script will recognize the speech, match it to the corresponding task, and print the appropriate response.

---

## Extending the Automation System

In a real-world application, the automate_task() function would be extended to interact with actual smart home devices. For example, you could integrate with APIs for IoT devices (e.g., smart light bulbs, thermostats) to perform actions like:

- **Turning on/off lights**: Using the phue library to control Philips Hue lights.
- **Adjusting the thermostat**: Using an API to interact with a smart thermostat like Nest.
- **Controlling other devices**: Using APIs for smart plugs, speakers, or other devices.

---

In this chapter, we explored how to integrate **speech recognition** into automation tasks using **Python** and libraries like **SpeechRecognition** and **PyAudio**. We built an automation system that listens for voice commands and performs tasks such as controlling smart home devices.

By automating tasks through voice commands, we enable hands-free operation of smart home devices, improving accessibility and convenience. This type of automation can be expanded to various domains, such as healthcare (automating patient monitoring systems), security (automating surveillance cameras), or business (automating workflows through voice commands).

The ability to integrate voice recognition into automation workflows opens up many possibilities, and with the help of Python and its libraries, it becomes easy to develop and deploy voice-controlled automation systems.

# Chapter 16: Building Chatbots with Python for Automation

## Introduction to Chatbots and Their Uses

Chatbots are automated systems that can simulate human conversation, typically through text or voice interactions. They are designed to assist users by providing instant responses to queries, automating tasks, and enhancing user engagement. Over the years, chatbots have become essential tools in various industries, helping businesses to streamline operations, improve customer service, and reduce the workload on human employees.

*Key Uses of Chatbots:*

1. **Customer Support**: Chatbots can provide 24/7 customer service by answering frequently asked questions, resolving common issues, and guiding users through troubleshooting steps.

2. **E-commerce**: Chatbots can assist with product recommendations, order tracking, and customer queries, leading to enhanced shopping experiences.

3. **Healthcare**: Chatbots can schedule appointments, provide medical advice, and assist in patient management by automating interactions with patients.

4. **Banking**: Chatbots can help users manage their accounts, perform transactions, and answer banking-related questions.

5. **HR and Recruitment**: Chatbots are used to screen resumes, schedule interviews, and answer employee queries related to HR policies.

The growth of chatbots in automation stems from their ability to handle repetitive tasks, offer personalized user experiences, and support scalability.

---

## Using Frameworks like ChatterBot and Rasa

Building an effective chatbot requires selecting the right framework. Several Python libraries and frameworks make it easy to create and deploy chatbots. Two popular options are **ChatterBot** and **Rasa**.

### *1. ChatterBot*

**ChatterBot** is an easy-to-use Python library for creating conversational chatbots. It uses machine learning algorithms to generate responses based on user input and can be trained on any conversational data.

- **Key Features of ChatterBot**:
    - Supports multiple languages.
    - Capable of learning from conversations, making it highly adaptable.
    - Can be trained with custom datasets or pre-existing data.
    - Requires minimal coding to build a basic chatbot.

**Installation**:

bash

pip install chatterbot chatterbot_corpus

**Example**: Basic chatbot using ChatterBot

python

```
from chatterbot import ChatBot
from chatterbot.trainers import ChatterBotCorpusTrainer

# Create a chatbot instance
chatbot = ChatBot('CustomerServiceBot')

# Train the chatbot with a predefined corpus
trainer = ChatterBotCorpusTrainer(chatbot)
trainer.train('chatterbot.corpus.english')

# Function to get a response from the chatbot
def get_response(user_input):
```

```
response = chatbot.get_response(user_input)
return response

# Start interacting with the chatbot
while True:
    user_input = input("You: ")
    if user_input.lower() == 'exit':
        break
    print("Bot: ", get_response(user_input))
```

This simple chatbot can interact with users based on the pre-trained corpus. It can be further enhanced by training the bot with custom data or integrating it with APIs for dynamic interactions.

## 2. Rasa

**Rasa** is a more advanced and powerful open-source framework for building chatbots and conversational AI systems. Unlike ChatterBot, which primarily focuses on generating responses based on training data, Rasa allows for more control over conversational flows, intents, and dialogue management.

- **Key Features of Rasa**:
    - Advanced natural language understanding (NLU) and dialogue management.
    - Customizable and scalable for complex applications.
    - Can integrate with APIs, databases, and messaging platforms.

o Supports advanced capabilities like context management and slot filling.

Rasa's architecture consists of two primary components:

- **Rasa NLU (Natural Language Understanding)**: Processes user input and extracts meaningful intents and entities.
- **Rasa Core**: Manages the conversation flow and logic based on predefined rules and stories.

**Installation**:

bash

pip install rasa

**Example**: Rasa chatbot setup typically involves defining intents, training data, and actions. The following steps will give a high-level overview of setting up Rasa for a customer service chatbot:

1. **Create a Rasa project**:

   bash

   rasa init

2. **Define Intents and Entities** in the nlu.md file, such as intents like greet, inform, ask_help.
3. **Create Stories** in stories.md to define possible conversation paths, such as user greetings or requests for assistance.

4. **Train the Model**:

```bash
```

```bash
rasa train
```

5. **Run the Bot**:

```bash
```

```bash
rasa shell
```

Rasa provides more flexibility and customization, making it suitable for complex, production-level chatbots.

---

# Example: Automating Customer Service with a Python-powered Chatbot

In this example, we will use **ChatterBot** to build a simple customer service chatbot. The chatbot will answer basic customer queries, like checking order status or providing contact information.

### Step 1: Install ChatterBot

If you haven't already installed ChatterBot and ChatterBot Corpus, use the following command:

```bash
```

```bash
pip install chatterbot chatterbot_corpus
```

## *Step 2: Create the Chatbot*

We will define a chatbot using ChatterBot, train it with a sample dataset (like English language corpus), and create a simple customer service interface for automated responses.

python

```python
from chatterbot import ChatBot
from chatterbot.trainers import ChatterBotCorpusTrainer

# Initialize the chatbot
chatbot = ChatBot('CustomerServiceBot')

# Create a trainer for the chatbot
trainer = ChatterBotCorpusTrainer(chatbot)

# Train the chatbot on the English corpus
trainer.train('chatterbot.corpus.english')

# Function to handle responses
def get_response(user_input):
    response = chatbot.get_response(user_input)
    return response

# Automating customer service: defining common customer queries
def customer_service_bot():
    print("Hello! I'm your Customer Service Assistant. How can I help you today?")

    while True:
```

```
user_input = input("You: ")

    # Simple exit condition
    if user_input.lower() in ['exit', 'quit', 'bye']:
        print("Bot: Goodbye!")
        break

    # Respond to the customer query
    response = get_response(user_input)
    print("Bot:", response)

# Start the chatbot
customer_service_bot()
```

### Step 3: Testing the Chatbot

After running the script, the chatbot will prompt the user for input. It can automatically respond to queries like:

- "How can I track my order?"
- "What is your return policy?"
- "Can you help me with a billing issue?"

This is a very basic example, but in real-world scenarios, you can expand the bot's capabilities by integrating it with your business database, customer management systems, or knowledge base to provide more specific and accurate responses.

## Extending the Chatbot for More Advanced Features

In a real-world deployment, you can expand this basic chatbot by adding more advanced features:

- **Personalization**: Store customer data, such as past orders or preferences, to make the bot more personalized.
- **Integration with APIs**: Connect the chatbot with external APIs (e.g., for order tracking, customer support ticketing).
- **Handling Context**: Use frameworks like **Rasa** to manage conversational context (e.g., knowing whether the user has asked for help before, or if they are still interacting with the same session).
- **Multilingual Support**: Train the bot to recognize and respond in multiple languages using additional language corpora.

---

In this chapter, we introduced **chatbots** and how they can be used to automate customer service and other tasks. We explored the basics of building a chatbot using **ChatterBot** and how it can be trained on predefined datasets. We also touched on more advanced chatbot frameworks like **Rasa**, which offer greater flexibility and control over conversational flows and integrations.

Building and automating customer service with a Python-powered chatbot is a powerful way to improve user engagement, reduce response time, and enhance customer satisfaction. Chatbots are not limited to customer service; they can be used in various other domains like healthcare, finance, and entertainment.

As you expand your chatbot projects, consider integrating more advanced NLP techniques, using machine learning models for dynamic responses, and creating more personalized and intelligent bots capable of managing more complex interactions.

# Chapter 17: Automating Web Interaction with Python

---

## Using Selenium to Automate Web Browsing Tasks

Web automation is a powerful tool that allows us to simulate user interactions with a website, such as filling out forms, clicking buttons, and navigating through pages. **Selenium** is one of the most popular Python libraries for automating web browsing tasks. It provides a simple interface for interacting with web elements and simulating actions such as clicks, text input, and even handling pop-ups.

Selenium supports multiple web browsers, including Chrome, Firefox, and Safari, and works across multiple platforms. It is widely used in areas like:

- **Web scraping**: Automating the process of extracting data from websites.
- **Testing**: Automating the testing of web applications to simulate real user interactions.
- **Task automation**: Automating repetitive tasks like form submissions, logging into websites, and navigating between pages.

## Key Features of Selenium

- **Browser Automation**: Selenium allows you to control web browsers programmatically, which means you can perform actions like clicking, typing, navigating, and even taking screenshots.
- **Element Locators**: Selenium provides a variety of ways to locate elements on a page, including **ID, class name, XPath**, and **CSS selectors**.
- **Waiting Mechanisms**: It supports both explicit and implicit waits to handle dynamic page content that may load at different times.
- **Cross-browser Support**: Selenium supports different browsers, such as Chrome, Firefox, Safari, and Internet Explorer.

## Installation of Selenium and WebDriver

To start using Selenium, you need to install the Selenium library and a WebDriver for the browser you plan to automate (e.g., ChromeDriver for Google Chrome).

1. **Install Selenium**:

bash

pip install selenium

2. **Install WebDriver**:

   o For **Google Chrome**, download the appropriate version of **ChromeDriver** from: ChromeDriver download.

   o For **Firefox**, download **GeckoDriver** from: GeckoDriver download.

   o Make sure that the driver is added to your system's PATH, or specify the path directly when initializing the browser in the code.

---

## Automating Web Interactions

With Selenium, you can automate various web interactions such as:

- **Filling out forms**: Inputting text, selecting options, and submitting forms.
- **Clicking buttons**: Simulating button clicks to navigate or submit forms.
- **Scraping data**: Extracting data from tables, forms, or other web elements.

- **Handling pop-ups and alerts**: Automating interactions with modal dialogs or alert boxes.

### *1. Opening a Browser and Navigating to a URL*

To begin automating web tasks with Selenium, you first need to initialize a browser session. The following example demonstrates how to open a browser, navigate to a webpage, and print the page title.

python

```
from selenium import webdriver

# Initialize the WebDriver (use the path to your driver if not set in PATH)
driver = webdriver.Chrome(executable_path='/path/to/chromedriver')

# Navigate to a webpage
driver.get('https://www.example.com')

# Print the page title
print(driver.title)

# Close the browser session
driver.quit()
```

This script will launch the Chrome browser, open the specified URL, and print the title of the webpage.

## *2. Filling Out Forms and Clicking Buttons*

Automating form submission is one of the most common use cases for Selenium. You can interact with input fields, select dropdown options, and click buttons.

python

```python
from selenium import webdriver
from selenium.webdriver.common.by import By
from selenium.webdriver.common.keys import Keys

# Initialize the WebDriver
driver = webdriver.Chrome(executable_path='/path/to/chromedriver')

# Navigate to a login page
driver.get('https://www.example.com/login')

# Find the input elements by their HTML tags or attributes
username = driver.find_element(By.NAME, 'username')
password = driver.find_element(By.NAME, 'password')

# Fill out the form by sending text to the input fields
username.send_keys('myusername')
password.send_keys('mypassword')

# Submit the form by pressing the Enter key
password.send_keys(Keys.RETURN)

# Alternatively, you can click a submit button
# login_button = driver.find_element(By.XPATH, '//button[@type="submit"]')
```

```
# login_button.click()

# Close the browser session
driver.quit()
```

In this example, we:

- Open a login page.
- Locate the username and password input fields using the find_element method.
- Send keys (the username and password) to the input fields.
- Simulate pressing the **Enter** key to submit the form.

### 3. Scraping Data from a Web Page

You can use Selenium to scrape data from a webpage by locating the elements and extracting their text or attributes. Here's how you can scrape data, such as extracting all product names from an e-commerce website:

python

```
from selenium import webdriver
from selenium.webdriver.common.by import By

# Initialize the WebDriver
driver = webdriver.Chrome(executable_path='/path/to/chromedriver')

# Navigate to an e-commerce page
driver.get('https://www.example.com/products')
```

```python
# Find the product elements by their class name
products = driver.find_elements(By.CLASS_NAME, 'product-name')

# Print the names of all products
for product in products:
    print(product.text)

# Close the browser session
driver.quit()
```

In this script, we:

- Locate all product name elements using find_elements with the class name product-name.
- Loop through the elements and print their text.

---

# Example: Automating Login and Data Submission on a Website

Let's build a more complete example: automating login and data submission on a website. In this case, we'll automate a login form, submit it, and fill out another form (e.g., feedback form) after login.

### Step 1: Set Up the Script for Logging In

We'll assume that the login page requires a username and password and that after logging in, the user needs to submit a feedback form.

python

```python
from selenium import webdriver
from selenium.webdriver.common.by import By
from selenium.webdriver.common.keys import Keys
import time

# Initialize the WebDriver
driver = webdriver.Chrome(executable_path='/path/to/chromedriver')

# Step 1: Log in to the website
driver.get('https://www.example.com/login')

# Find and fill in the username and password fields
username = driver.find_element(By.NAME, 'username')
password = driver.find_element(By.NAME, 'password')

username.send_keys('myusername')
password.send_keys('mypassword')
password.send_keys(Keys.RETURN)  # Press Enter to log in

# Wait for the login to complete
time.sleep(2)  # Wait for 2 seconds (adjust if necessary)

# Step 2: Navigate to the feedback page (assuming it requires login)
driver.get('https://www.example.com/feedback')

# Step 3: Fill out the feedback form
feedback_field = driver.find_element(By.NAME, 'feedback')
submit_button = driver.find_element(By.NAME, 'submit')
```

```
feedback_field.send_keys('This is my feedback.')
submit_button.click()

# Wait for the form submission to complete
time.sleep(2)

# Print confirmation message or any other relevant output
print("Form submitted successfully!")

# Close the browser session
driver.quit()
```

## *Explanation of the Code:*

1. **Login**: We open the login page, locate the username and password fields, input the credentials, and submit the form by simulating pressing the **Enter** key.
2. **Navigate to Feedback Page**: After logging in, we navigate to a feedback page.
3. **Fill Out the Feedback Form**: We find the feedback field, enter some text, and click the submit button to submit the form.
4. **Automation Logic**: The entire process is automated, and after the form is submitted, we close the browser session.

In this chapter, we explored how to automate web interactions using **Selenium**. We covered the basics of opening a browser, navigating to a webpage, and automating interactions such as:

- Filling out forms.
- Clicking buttons.
- Scraping data from web pages.
- Handling logins and submitting data.

Selenium's flexibility and powerful features make it an excellent tool for automating repetitive web tasks, conducting automated testing, and scraping data from websites. This kind of automation is used in areas such as web scraping, automated testing, and even automating user interactions on web platforms.

As you progress, you can integrate more complex scenarios, such as handling dynamic content, dealing with pop-ups, automating multi-step workflows, and integrating Selenium with databases or APIs to process the data further.

# Chapter 18: Automating Data Analysis and Reporting with Python

## Using Python for Automated Data Analysis Tasks

Data analysis is a critical part of many business operations, research, and decision-making processes. Automating data analysis tasks helps save time, reduce human error, and streamline workflows. Python provides a wide range of libraries for data manipulation, analysis, and visualization that make it an ideal tool for automating these tasks.

In this chapter, we will explore how to use Python for automating data analysis tasks, focusing on key libraries like **pandas**, **Matplotlib**, and **Seaborn**. These libraries help with data manipulation, statistical analysis, and visualization, respectively. We will also go through an example of automating financial reporting using Python, which involves reading financial data, performing calculations, and generating visual reports.

## Key Libraries for Data Analysis in Python

### 1. pandas

**pandas** is the cornerstone library for data manipulation and analysis in Python. It provides data structures such as **DataFrame** and **Series**, which allow for efficient handling of large datasets, including operations like filtering, aggregation, and merging.

- **DataFrames**: A 2-dimensional labeled data structure, similar to a table or spreadsheet, with rows and columns.
- **Series**: A 1-dimensional labeled array used for storing a single column of data.

**Common Tasks with pandas**:

- Importing and exporting data (CSV, Excel, JSON, etc.).
- Cleaning and transforming data (handling missing values, applying functions).
- Grouping, aggregating, and summarizing data.
- Merging and joining different datasets.

**Installation**:

bash

pip install pandas

## 2. Matplotlib

**Matplotlib** is a comprehensive library for creating static, animated, and interactive visualizations in Python. It is the most widely used library for plotting in Python and is the foundation for other libraries like **Seaborn** and **pandas** plotting.

**Common Tasks with Matplotlib**:

- Creating line plots, bar charts, histograms, and scatter plots.
- Customizing plot labels, titles, and legends.
- Saving visualizations as images or interactive plots.

**Installation**:

bash

pip install matplotlib

### 3. Seaborn

**Seaborn** is built on top of Matplotlib and provides a high-level interface for drawing attractive and informative statistical graphics. It simplifies the creation of complex visualizations like heatmaps, pair plots, and violin plots, and is particularly useful for visualizing categorical data and distributions.

**Common Tasks with Seaborn**:

- Statistical plots like box plots, histograms, and density plots.
- Plotting relationships between variables using scatter plots and line plots.
- Visualizing complex data distributions with a few lines of code.

**Installation**:

bash

pip install seaborn

---

## Automating Data Analysis with Python

Now that we've introduced the key libraries, let's walk through an example of automating a data analysis task. In this case, we'll automate **financial reporting**, which involves:

- Loading financial data (such as revenue, expenses, and profits).
- Calculating summary statistics.
- Visualizing the results using graphs.
- Generating a report.

### *Step 1: Install Required Libraries*
Ensure that you have **pandas**, **Matplotlib**, and **Seaborn** installed.

bash

pip install pandas matplotlib seaborn

### *Step 2: Load Financial Data*
For this example, we will use a CSV file containing financial data for a company. The file contains columns such as **Month, Revenue,**

**Expenses**, and **Profit**. You can adjust this example to fit the actual structure of your data.

python

```python
import pandas as pd

# Load the financial data from a CSV file
data = pd.read_csv('financial_data.csv')

# Display the first few rows of the data
print(data.head())
```

The CSV file might look like this:

plaintext

```plaintext
Month,Revenue,Expenses,Profit
January,100000,50000,50000
February,120000,60000,60000
March,110000,55000,55000
April,115000,58000,57000
```

## *Step 3: Perform Calculations*

We will calculate key financial metrics, such as:

- **Total Revenue**: The sum of all revenues.
- **Total Expenses**: The sum of all expenses.
- **Total Profit**: The sum of all profits.

python

```python
# Calculate total revenue, expenses, and profit
total_revenue = data['Revenue'].sum()
total_expenses = data['Expenses'].sum()
total_profit = data['Profit'].sum()

# Print the summary
print(f"Total Revenue: {total_revenue}")
print(f"Total Expenses: {total_expenses}")
print(f"Total Profit: {total_profit}")
```

## *Step 4: Visualize the Financial Data*

Next, we will visualize the financial data using **Matplotlib** and **Seaborn**. We will create a line plot to show the trend of revenue, expenses, and profit over time, as well as a bar plot for the monthly breakdown.

python

```python
import matplotlib.pyplot as plt
import seaborn as sns

# Set the style of the plots
sns.set(style="whitegrid")

# Create a figure for the plots
plt.figure(figsize=(10, 6))

# Plot revenue, expenses, and profit
plt.plot(data['Month'], data['Revenue'], label='Revenue', marker='o', color='b')
```

```
plt.plot(data['Month'], data['Expenses'], label='Expenses', marker='o', color='r')
plt.plot(data['Month'], data['Profit'], label='Profit', marker='o', color='g')

# Adding titles and labels
plt.title('Financial Overview (Monthly)', fontsize=14)
plt.xlabel('Month', fontsize=12)
plt.ylabel('Amount (in USD)', fontsize=12)
plt.xticks(rotation=45)
plt.legend()

# Show the plot
plt.tight_layout()
plt.show()

# Create a bar plot for revenue vs. expenses vs. profit
data.set_index('Month')[['Revenue',    'Expenses',    'Profit']].plot(kind='bar',
figsize=(10, 6))

# Adding title
plt.title('Monthly Financial Breakdown', fontsize=14)
plt.ylabel('Amount (in USD)', fontsize=12)
plt.xticks(rotation=45)
plt.tight_layout()
plt.show()
```

In this code:

- **Line Plot**: We visualize the trend of revenue, expenses, and profit over time.

- **Bar Plot**: We create a bar plot that shows the monthly breakdown of revenue, expenses, and profit.

### *Step 5: Generate and Save the Report*

Finally, we can automate the generation of a financial report by combining the calculations and visualizations into a PDF or HTML file. Here's an example of how to generate a PDF report using **Matplotlib** and **pandas**.

python

```python
from matplotlib.backends.backend_pdf import PdfPages


# Create a PDF file to save the report
with PdfPages('financial_report.pdf') as pdf:
    # Plot the line chart and save it
    plt.figure(figsize=(10, 6))
    plt.plot(data['Month'], data['Revenue'], label='Revenue', marker='o', color='b')
    plt.plot(data['Month'], data['Expenses'], label='Expenses', marker='o', color='r')
    plt.plot(data['Month'], data['Profit'], label='Profit', marker='o', color='g')
    plt.title('Financial Overview (Monthly)', fontsize=14)
    plt.xlabel('Month', fontsize=12)
    plt.ylabel('Amount (in USD)', fontsize=12)
    plt.xticks(rotation=45)
    plt.legend()
    pdf.savefig()  # Save the current figure
    plt.close()


    # Plot the bar chart and save it
```

```
data.set_index('Month')[['Revenue',    'Expenses',    'Profit']].plot(kind='bar',
figsize=(10, 6))
    plt.title('Monthly Financial Breakdown', fontsize=14)
    plt.ylabel('Amount (in USD)', fontsize=12)
    plt.xticks(rotation=45)
    pdf.savefig()  # Save the current figure
    plt.close()


    # Add a text summary to the report
    from io import StringIO
    summary = StringIO()
    summary.write(f"Total Revenue: {total_revenue}\n")
    summary.write(f"Total Expenses: {total_expenses}\n")
    summary.write(f"Total Profit: {total_profit}\n")


    # Write the summary to a page in the PDF
    from matplotlib import pyplot as plt
    plt.figure(figsize=(8, 6))
    plt.text(0.5, 0.5, summary.getvalue(), ha='center', va='center', fontsize=12)
    plt.axis('off')
    pdf.savefig()
    plt.close()
```

This script will generate a PDF report containing:

- A line chart showing the trend of revenue, expenses, and profit.
- A bar chart showing the monthly breakdown.
- A summary of the total revenue, expenses, and profit.

In this chapter, we demonstrated how to use Python for **automated data analysis and reporting**. We explored how to leverage powerful libraries like **pandas** for data manipulation, **Matplotlib** for visualization, and **Seaborn** for advanced statistical graphics. By automating financial reporting tasks, we can quickly analyze data, visualize trends, and generate professional reports without manual intervention.

This approach can be extended to a variety of industries and use cases, including sales reports, performance tracking, and customer analytics. The ability to automate these tasks with Python increases efficiency, reduces human error, and frees up valuable time for other tasks.

As you continue to explore data automation, you can extend these techniques to more complex datasets, integrate with external APIs, and even automate predictive modeling and machine learning workflows to enhance your reporting capabilities.

# Chapter 19: AI-Powered Automation for Business Operations

## Implementing AI and Automation in Business Processes

In today's fast-paced business environment, organizations are increasingly turning to **Artificial Intelligence (AI)** and **automation** to streamline operations, reduce costs, and improve efficiency. By integrating AI-driven solutions into business processes, companies can handle repetitive tasks, make better data-driven decisions, and enhance overall productivity.

AI-powered automation is not limited to just one industry; it spans across various sectors such as manufacturing, retail, healthcare, finance, and logistics. It can assist in decision-making, optimize workflows, and enable businesses to focus more on strategic initiatives rather than manual tasks.

In this chapter, we will explore how AI can be integrated into business operations to automate processes. We will focus on common business tasks that can be automated, like **inventory management**, **scheduling**, and **order fulfillment**. Additionally, we will walk through an example of **automating order fulfillment using AI**.

# Streamlining Tasks Like Inventory Management and Scheduling

## 1. Automating Inventory Management

Inventory management is a critical function for any business that deals with physical products. Keeping track of stock levels, managing orders, and forecasting demand can be time-consuming and prone to errors when done manually. AI can help automate many of these processes, including:

- **Demand forecasting**: AI models can predict future product demand based on historical sales data, seasonal trends, and external factors.
- **Stock level monitoring**: AI can automatically monitor inventory levels and trigger reorder requests when stock is low.
- **Order processing**: AI can automate the process of checking stock levels and placing orders with suppliers when inventory is running low.
- **Supply chain optimization**: AI can help optimize the supply chain by selecting the best suppliers, determining the most efficient shipping routes, and forecasting delivery times.

**Tools for AI-powered Inventory Management**:

- **Machine learning models**: Predictive models that can forecast demand and suggest optimal stock levels.
- **IoT and sensors**: Internet of Things (IoT) devices can be used to track real-time stock levels and automate restocking.
- **Robotic Process Automation (RPA)**: Bots can automate manual data entry tasks and trigger workflows like reordering supplies when stock levels fall below a threshold.

## 2. Automating Scheduling

Scheduling is another area where AI can provide significant benefits. For businesses that rely on appointments, meetings, or shifts, managing schedules manually can be inefficient. AI-powered scheduling tools can automate the process by considering factors like availability, preferences, and priorities.

- **Appointment scheduling**: AI tools like chatbots can handle appointment bookings with customers by understanding the available time slots and customer preferences.
- **Employee scheduling**: AI can be used to generate optimized shift schedules based on employee availability, historical trends, and labor laws.
- **Resource allocation**: AI can help allocate resources, such as meeting rooms, equipment, or human resources, efficiently based on requirements.

**Tools for AI-powered Scheduling**:

- **Natural Language Processing (NLP)**: Used in AI chatbots that understand user queries and schedule appointments automatically.
- **Optimization algorithms**: AI algorithms can generate optimal schedules by balancing workload, employee preferences, and business requirements.

---

# Example: Automating Order Fulfillment Using AI

Order fulfillment is a critical part of the e-commerce and retail industries. It involves multiple tasks, including order processing, inventory checks, packaging, and shipping. Automating order fulfillment with AI can drastically reduce the time it takes to process orders and minimize human error.

In this example, we will automate a simplified order fulfillment process using AI. We will focus on the following steps:

- **Order Reception**: Automatically receiving an order from a customer.
- **Inventory Check**: Verifying product availability in the inventory.
- **Order Processing**: Preparing the order for shipment.

- **Shipping**: Sending the order to the customer using an optimized shipping route.

## Step 1: Install Necessary Libraries

We will use **pandas** for managing data, **random** for simulating stock availability, and a simple **AI algorithm** to check product availability.

bash

```
pip install pandas
```

## Step 2: Simulate Inventory and Orders

First, let's create a dataset for inventory and simulate receiving an order. The inventory will contain product names, stock quantities, and the prices of products.

python

```python
import pandas as pd
import random

# Create an inventory DataFrame
inventory = pd.DataFrame({
    'Product': ['Laptop', 'Smartphone', 'Headphones', 'Smartwatch', 'Tablet'],
    'Stock': [10, 20, 15, 30, 12],
    'Price': [1000, 800, 150, 250, 500]
})

# Simulate receiving an order
```

```python
def receive_order():
    # Randomly select a product and quantity
    product = random.choice(inventory['Product'])
    quantity = random.randint(1, 5)

    return product, quantity

# Example order
product, quantity = receive_order()
print(f"Received Order: {quantity} x {product}")
```

## Step 3: Check Inventory Availability Using AI

Now, we will automate the inventory check. If the ordered product is in stock, the system will process the order; otherwise, it will suggest a restock.

python

```python
def check_inventory(product, quantity):
    # Check if the product is in stock
    product_stock = inventory[inventory['Product'] == product]['Stock'].values[0]

    if product_stock >= quantity:
        # If sufficient stock, process the order
        print(f"Order processed: {quantity} x {product} available in stock.")
        return True
    else:
        # If stock is insufficient, suggest a restock
        print(f"Insufficient stock: Only {product_stock} x {product} available.")
        return False
```

```
# Check if the order can be fulfilled
order_fulfilled = check_inventory(product, quantity)
```

## Step 4: Process the Order and Automate Shipping

If the inventory check passes, we will simulate processing the order and then suggest a shipping route.

python

```python
def process_order(product, quantity):
    if order_fulfilled:
        # Process the order
        print(f"Processing {quantity} x {product} for shipping.")
        # Simulate shipping process
        shipping_cost = random.randint(5, 20)  # Random shipping cost
        print(f"Shipping cost: ${shipping_cost}")
        print("Order is on its way!")
    else:
        print("Order cannot be processed due to insufficient stock.")


# Process the order and automate shipping
process_order(product, quantity)
```

## Step 5: Integrate AI for Predictive Restocking

Now, let's add a simple **AI model** to predict when to reorder stock based on historical sales data. For simplicity, we can simulate demand prediction using random numbers. In a real-world scenario, this could be done using more sophisticated machine learning models.

python

```python
def predict_demand(product):
    # Simulate predicting future demand (e.g., based on historical data)
    predicted_demand = random.randint(5, 15)
    print(f"Predicted demand for {product}: {predicted_demand}")

    # Check if current stock is enough to meet predicted demand
    current_stock = inventory[inventory['Product'] == product]['Stock'].values[0]

    if current_stock < predicted_demand:
        print(f"Warning: Stock is insufficient for predicted demand. Consider restocking.")
    else:
        print(f"Stock level is sufficient to meet predicted demand.")

# Predict demand for the ordered product
predict_demand(product)
```

---

In this chapter, we explored how **AI-powered automation** can be applied to business operations to streamline tasks like **inventory management**, **scheduling**, and **order fulfillment**. We demonstrated how simple AI models can automate repetitive tasks, such as checking stock levels, processing orders, and predicting future demand.

By integrating AI into business processes, companies can:

- Improve operational efficiency by automating time-consuming tasks.
- Make data-driven decisions, such as predicting demand and managing stock levels.
- Reduce human error, ensuring more accurate and reliable processes.
- Enhance customer satisfaction by automating faster order fulfillment and response times.

As businesses continue to embrace AI, the opportunities for automation across various industries will grow. From manufacturing to customer service and logistics, AI-powered automation is becoming a game-changer for business operations.

# Chapter 20: Cloud Automation with Python

Introduction to Cloud Platforms like AWS, GCP, and
Azure

Cloud computing has revolutionized the way businesses operate, providing scalable, on-demand computing resources over the internet. Major cloud platforms such as **Amazon Web Services (AWS)**, **Google Cloud Platform (GCP)**, and **Microsoft Azure** have become the backbone of modern infrastructure, allowing organizations to scale their applications without worrying about maintaining physical hardware.

These cloud platforms offer a wide variety of services, including computing power, storage, networking, and machine learning capabilities. One of the key advantages of using cloud platforms is their ability to automate various tasks, which significantly reduces operational overhead and improves productivity.

*1. AWS (Amazon Web Services)*
AWS is one of the most popular cloud platforms, offering a broad range of services, including:

- **Compute**: EC2 (Elastic Compute Cloud), Lambda

- **Storage**: S3 (Simple Storage Service), EBS (Elastic Block Store)
- **Databases**: RDS (Relational Database Service), DynamoDB
- **Networking**: VPC (Virtual Private Cloud), Route 53

## 2. GCP (Google Cloud Platform)

GCP is another leading cloud platform, widely recognized for its strong offerings in AI, machine learning, and big data. Key services include:

- **Compute**: Compute Engine, Cloud Functions
- **Storage**: Cloud Storage, Persistent Disks
- **Big Data**: BigQuery, Dataflow
- **Networking**: VPC, Load Balancing

## 3. Azure

Microsoft Azure is known for its integration with Microsoft products and services, providing solutions across various industries:

- **Compute**: Virtual Machines, Azure Functions
- **Storage**: Blob Storage, Disk Storage
- **Databases**: Azure SQL Database, Cosmos DB
- **Networking**: Virtual Network, Azure Traffic Manager

# Automating Cloud Resource Management with Python SDKs

Cloud platforms provide Python SDKs (Software Development Kits) that allow developers to automate and manage cloud resources programmatically. These SDKs expose APIs that allow Python code to interact with cloud services, enabling tasks such as:

- Creating and managing virtual machines.
- Automating the provisioning of storage resources.
- Managing network configurations and security groups.
- Automating backup and recovery processes.

## *1. AWS SDK for Python: Boto3*

**Boto3** is the AWS SDK for Python, and it allows developers to automate AWS service management. With Boto3, you can interact with AWS services like EC2, S3, RDS, and more.

**Key Features of Boto3**:

- Manage EC2 instances (start, stop, create, terminate).
- Upload and download files to/from S3.
- Manage DynamoDB tables and RDS instances.
- Automate Lambda functions and more.

**Installation**:

bash

```
pip install boto3
```

## 2. Google Cloud SDK for Python

Google Cloud offers the **google-cloud** library, which provides APIs for interacting with GCP services. With this SDK, you can automate tasks like deploying applications, managing resources, and using machine learning models.

### Installation:

bash

```
pip install google-cloud
```

## 3. Azure SDK for Python

Azure's **azure-sdk-for-python** allows you to interact with Azure services programmatically. It supports services like Azure Storage, Azure Virtual Machines, and Azure Active Directory.

### Installation:

bash

```
pip install azure-mgmt-resource azure-storage-blob
```

---

# Example: Automating Cloud Storage Management Using Boto3 on AWS

In this example, we will automate the management of **Amazon S3** (Simple Storage Service) using **Boto3**. We will focus on the following tasks:

- Uploading a file to an S3 bucket.
- Downloading a file from an S3 bucket.
- Listing the files in an S3 bucket.
- Deleting a file from an S3 bucket.

### Step 1: Set Up AWS Credentials

Before using Boto3, you need to configure AWS credentials on your system. You can set up credentials using the AWS CLI or manually by placing them in the ~/.aws/credentials file. Here's the basic structure for the credentials file:

plaintext

```
[default]
aws_access_key_id = YOUR_ACCESS_KEY
aws_secret_access_key = YOUR_SECRET_KEY
region = YOUR_AWS_REGION
```

### Step 2: Install Boto3

bash

```
pip install boto3
```

### Step 3: Automate S3 Operations

The following script demonstrates how to automate common S3 tasks using Boto3.

python

```python
import boto3
from botocore.exceptions import NoCredentialsError

# Initialize the S3 client
s3 = boto3.client('s3')

# Step 1: Upload a file to S3
def upload_file(file_name, bucket_name, object_name=None):
    try:
        if object_name is None:
            object_name = file_name
        s3.upload_file(file_name, bucket_name, object_name)
        print(f"File '{file_name}' uploaded to '{bucket_name}/{object_name}'")
    except NoCredentialsError:
        print("Credentials not available")

# Step 2: Download a file from S3
def download_file(bucket_name, object_name, file_name):
    try:
        s3.download_file(bucket_name, object_name, file_name)
        print(f"File '{object_name}' downloaded from '{bucket_name}' to '{file_name}'")
    except NoCredentialsError:
        print("Credentials not available")
```

```python
# Step 3: List files in an S3 bucket
def list_files(bucket_name):
    try:
        response = s3.list_objects_v2(Bucket=bucket_name)
        print("Files in S3 bucket:")
        for obj in response.get('Contents', []):
            print(f" - {obj['Key']}")
    except NoCredentialsError:
        print("Credentials not available")


# Step 4: Delete a file from S3
def delete_file(bucket_name, object_name):
    try:
        s3.delete_object(Bucket=bucket_name, Key=object_name)
        print(f"File '{object_name}' deleted from '{bucket_name}'")
    except NoCredentialsError:
        print("Credentials not available")


# Example usage
bucket_name = 'your-bucket-name'
file_to_upload = 'local_file.txt'
object_name = 'uploaded_file.txt'


# Upload a file
upload_file(file_to_upload, bucket_name, object_name)


# List files in the bucket
list_files(bucket_name)


# Download a file
```

download_file(bucket_name, object_name, 'downloaded_file.txt')

# Delete a file
delete_file(bucket_name, object_name)

## *Explanation of the Code:*

1. **Upload File**: The upload_file function uploads a file to a specified S3 bucket.

2. **Download File**: The download_file function downloads a file from the S3 bucket to a local file.

3. **List Files**: The list_files function lists all objects in a given S3 bucket.

4. **Delete File**: The delete_file function deletes a file from the S3 bucket.

## *Step 4: Run the Script*

Before running the script, ensure that you have:

- Created an S3 bucket on AWS.
- Stored the correct AWS access keys in your configuration file or environment variables.

When you run the script, it will:

1. Upload a file (local_file.txt) to the S3 bucket.
2. List all files in the bucket.
3. Download the uploaded file.

4. Delete the uploaded file.

---

In this chapter, we discussed the benefits and capabilities of using **AI-powered automation** for cloud resource management, focusing on popular cloud platforms like **AWS**, **GCP**, and **Azure**. We then delved into automating cloud storage management using **Boto3**, the AWS SDK for Python.

By leveraging cloud platforms and Python SDKs, businesses can automate a wide range of tasks, including resource provisioning, monitoring, data storage management, and scaling. This leads to increased efficiency, reduced operational costs, and the ability to scale infrastructure as needed.

The example demonstrated automating file management tasks using AWS S3, such as uploading, downloading, listing, and deleting files. This is just a starting point—cloud automation can extend to provisioning EC2 instances, managing databases, deploying machine learning models, and more.

# Chapter 21: Integrating Python with IoT for Automation

## Connecting Python with IoT Devices for Automation

The Internet of Things (IoT) refers to the network of physical devices embedded with sensors, software, and other technologies, enabling them to collect, exchange, and act on data. IoT devices are widely used in smart homes, industrial automation, healthcare, agriculture, and other sectors.

Python is an excellent programming language for working with IoT devices due to its simplicity, ease of integration with hardware, and vast ecosystem of libraries. By connecting Python with IoT devices, we can automate tasks, gather data from sensors, control actuators, and create smart systems.

In this chapter, we will discuss how to integrate Python with IoT devices, using libraries and tools for communication between the software and hardware components. We will also walk through an example of automating smart home tasks, such as controlling lights and monitoring temperature, with Python.

## Libraries and Tools for IoT Integration

Python offers several libraries and tools that make it easy to connect with and control IoT devices. Here are some key libraries commonly used for IoT projects:

### 1. GPIO (General Purpose Input/Output)

The **RPi.GPIO** library allows Python to control the GPIO pins on Raspberry Pi boards. This is ideal for interacting with sensors, switches, motors, and other peripherals connected to the Raspberry Pi.

**Installation**:

bash

pip install RPi.GPIO

### 2. PySerial

**PySerial** is a Python library that provides a way to communicate with IoT devices via serial ports (e.g., connecting an Arduino board or a sensor that uses serial communication).

**Installation**:

bash

pip install pyserial

### 3. MQTT (Message Queuing Telemetry Transport)

**MQTT** is a lightweight messaging protocol designed for IoT. It is ideal for sending small messages between devices over low-bandwidth or unreliable networks. The **paho-mqtt** library enables Python applications to connect to MQTT brokers and publish/subscribe to topics.

**Installation**:

bash

pip install paho-mqtt

## 4. Flask

**Flask** is a micro web framework for Python. It is often used for building RESTful APIs that can control IoT devices. With Flask, you can create web-based interfaces to interact with IoT devices.

**Installation**:

bash

pip install Flask

## 5. Home Assistant

**Home Assistant** is an open-source platform for automating smart home devices. It supports a wide range of IoT devices and integrates well with Python. Python scripts can be used to extend Home Assistant's functionality.

**Installation**:

bash

pip install homeassistant

---

## Example: Automating Smart Home Tasks with Python

In this example, we will simulate a basic smart home system using Python. We will automate the following tasks:

- **Turning on/off lights** using a Raspberry Pi and GPIO.
- **Monitoring temperature** using a temperature sensor connected to the Raspberry Pi.
- **Sending notifications** using an MQTT broker when the temperature exceeds a certain threshold.

### *Step 1: Setting Up Hardware (Simulated)*

For this example, we'll simulate a Raspberry Pi environment using Python. You can adapt this code for real-world IoT devices such as the Raspberry Pi, Arduino, or ESP32.

- **Light Control**: Simulate controlling a light using a GPIO pin on the Raspberry Pi.
- **Temperature Monitoring**: Simulate reading a temperature sensor value (e.g., DHT11) and send notifications when the temperature exceeds a threshold.

### *Step 2: Install Necessary Libraries*

Make sure you have installed the necessary libraries for IoT integration.

bash

```
pip install RPi.GPIO paho-mqtt
```

### Step 3: Simulate the Smart Home System with Python

Let's write a Python script to simulate controlling lights and monitoring temperature using an IoT platform.

python

```python
import time
import RPi.GPIO as GPIO
import paho.mqtt.client as mqtt

# Set up the GPIO pin for controlling the light (simulated)
LIGHT_PIN = 17  # Use GPIO pin 17 for the light control
GPIO.setmode(GPIO.BCM)  # Set the pin numbering system
GPIO.setup(LIGHT_PIN, GPIO.OUT)  # Set the pin as an output

# Set up MQTT client
broker = "mqtt.eclipse.org"  # MQTT broker (public broker)
port = 1883  # MQTT port
topic = "home/temperature"  # Topic for temperature updates

# Temperature threshold for automation
TEMPERATURE_THRESHOLD = 30  # Temperature in Celsius
```

```python
# MQTT callback functions
def on_connect(client, userdata, flags, rc):
    print("Connected to MQTT broker with result code " + str(rc))


def on_message(client, userdata, msg):
    # Parse the message
    temperature = float(msg.payload.decode())
    print(f"Received temperature: {temperature}°C")

    # Check if the temperature exceeds the threshold
    if temperature > TEMPERATURE_THRESHOLD:
        print("Temperature exceeds threshold! Turning on the fan.")
        client.publish("home/fan", "ON")  # Send command to turn on fan


# Set up the MQTT client and connect to the broker
client = mqtt.Client()
client.on_connect = on_connect
client.on_message = on_message
client.connect(broker, port, 60)
client.subscribe("home/temperature")  # Subscribe to temperature updates


# Simulate controlling the light (turning on/off)
def control_light(command):
    if command == "ON":
        GPIO.output(LIGHT_PIN, GPIO.HIGH)  # Turn on the light
        print("Light turned ON.")
    elif command == "OFF":
        GPIO.output(LIGHT_PIN, GPIO.LOW)  # Turn off the light
        print("Light turned OFF.")
```

```python
# Simulate monitoring the temperature (in reality, use a sensor)
def monitor_temperature():
    while True:
        # Simulate a random temperature value (between 25°C and 35°C)
        simulated_temperature = 25 + (time.time() % 10)
        print(f"Simulated Temperature: {simulated_temperature}°C")

        # Send the temperature value to the MQTT broker
        client.publish("home/temperature", simulated_temperature)

        # Wait before checking again
        time.sleep(5)

# Main logic for automating tasks
if __name__ == "__main__":
    try:
        # Start the MQTT client loop in a separate thread
        client.loop_start()

        # Simulate controlling the light based on a condition
        control_light("ON")
        time.sleep(3)
        control_light("OFF")

        # Monitor the temperature continuously
        monitor_temperature()

    except KeyboardInterrupt:
        print("Exiting the program.")
        GPIO.cleanup()  # Clean up GPIO settings
```

client.loop_stop()  # Stop the MQTT loop

## *Step 4: Explanation of the Code*

1. **GPIO Light Control**: We simulate controlling a light connected to GPIO pin 17 on a Raspberry Pi. The control_light() function turns the light on and off based on the command received.

2. **Temperature Monitoring**: The monitor_temperature() function simulates reading temperature data. In a real-world scenario, you would use a temperature sensor (e.g., DHT11 or DS18B20) to get actual readings.

3. **MQTT Communication**: We use the **MQTT protocol** for communication between the IoT devices. The on_message() callback checks the received temperature and triggers an action if it exceeds the predefined threshold (e.g., turning on the fan).

4. **Automation Logic**: The system controls the light and monitors the temperature continuously. It also sends temperature updates to an MQTT broker, which can be subscribed to by other devices.

## *Step 5: Test the System*

- Start the Python script. It will simulate controlling the light and monitor the temperature.

- The system will continuously send simulated temperature values to the MQTT broker.
- If the temperature exceeds the threshold, a message will be sent to turn on the fan (simulated).

In this chapter, we explored how to **integrate Python with IoT devices** for automation. Python provides a range of libraries and tools that make it easy to interface with IoT hardware and automate tasks. We focused on automating smart home tasks, including controlling lights and monitoring temperature, using the **RPi.GPIO** and **paho-mqtt** libraries.

IoT automation can improve efficiency, convenience, and reliability in many different applications, from home automation to industrial processes. By connecting Python to IoT devices, you can create smart systems that autonomously monitor and control the physical world. Whether you are building a simple smart home system or a complex industrial automation solution, Python is an excellent tool for developing scalable and effective IoT solutions.

# Chapter 22: Automation with Python in Data Engineering

---

## Automating ETL (Extract, Transform, Load) Processes

In the world of **data engineering**, one of the most fundamental tasks is the automation of the **ETL process**. ETL stands for **Extract, Transform**, and **Load**, which are the three core steps involved in preparing data for analysis or storage. Automating this process is crucial for improving efficiency, reducing manual effort, and ensuring that data flows seamlessly from various sources into a data warehouse or analysis environment.

### 1. What is ETL?

- **Extract**: This is the process of retrieving data from various sources, such as databases, APIs, files (e.g., CSV, Excel), and web scraping. The data might be in different formats and from diverse systems.
- **Transform**: In this step, the extracted data is cleaned, filtered, aggregated, or formatted. This might involve removing duplicate values, handling missing data, performing calculations, or converting the data into a consistent format.

- **Load**: After transforming the data, it is loaded into a target system such as a database, data warehouse, or a file system, where it can be analyzed or used by other applications.

Automating the ETL process involves writing scripts that handle these tasks on a schedule or in response to certain triggers. Python is widely used for ETL automation due to its rich ecosystem of libraries and frameworks that simplify these processes.

---

## Using Python for Data Pipelines and Automation

Python provides a number of libraries and frameworks that can be used to build and automate data pipelines. These pipelines help streamline the ETL process and ensure that data flows smoothly between systems. Some popular Python libraries for data engineering include:

### 1. pandas

**pandas** is one of the most widely used libraries for data manipulation and analysis. It offers powerful tools for handling structured data (e.g., CSV, Excel, SQL) and is commonly used in the **Transform** step of the ETL process.

- **Extract**: pandas can read data from various sources, including CSV, Excel, and SQL databases.

- **Transform**: pandas offers tools for cleaning, transforming, and analyzing data, such as handling missing data, filtering, and aggregating.
- **Load**: pandas can write data back to different formats, such as CSV, Excel, or SQL databases.

## 2. Airflow

**Apache Airflow** is an open-source platform used to orchestrate complex workflows and schedule tasks. It is commonly used for automating ETL workflows, including the scheduling and monitoring of data pipelines.

- **Task Scheduling**: Airflow allows you to schedule and monitor ETL tasks with its rich scheduling and execution engine.
- **Pipeline Orchestration**: You can define workflows using Python code to manage dependencies and execute steps in a specific order.
- **Error Handling**: Airflow allows you to handle failures and retries, ensuring robust and resilient pipelines.

## 3. SQLAlchemy

**SQLAlchemy** is a Python SQL toolkit that facilitates database interactions. It helps you connect to relational databases, execute SQL queries, and manage the transfer of data.

- **Extract**: You can use SQLAlchemy to connect to relational databases and extract data.
- **Load**: After transforming the data, SQLAlchemy can be used to load the data back into a database.

### 4. Dask

**Dask** is a Python library for parallel computing, making it ideal for handling large datasets that don't fit into memory. It can be used to scale data pipelines across multiple cores or machines.

- **ETL Automation**: Dask helps in processing large datasets in parallel, making the ETL process faster and more efficient.

### 5. Prefect

**Prefect** is a modern data workflow orchestration tool, similar to Airflow, but with a simpler API. It is designed to handle the orchestration, scheduling, and monitoring of data pipelines with ease.

---

# Example: Building an Automated Data Pipeline for Analysis

Let's walk through an example of building a basic automated data pipeline that reads data from a CSV file, transforms the data, and loads it into a database for further analysis. In this example, we will:

1. Extract data from a CSV file.

2. Perform transformations like data cleaning and filtering.

3. Load the transformed data into an SQLite database.

### *Step 1: Install Necessary Libraries*

We will use the following libraries for this example:

- **pandas**: For data manipulation.

- **SQLAlchemy**: For database interaction.

bash

```
pip install pandas sqlalchemy sqlite3
```

### *Step 2: Extract Data from a CSV File*

We will begin by extracting data from a CSV file using pandas. The CSV file contains customer data with columns like Name, Age, Email, and Country.

python

```
import pandas as pd

# Extract data from CSV file
data = pd.read_csv('customers.csv')

# Display the first few rows of the data
print(data.head())
```

Example CSV content:

plaintext

Name, Age, Email, Country
Alice, 30, alice@example.com, USA
Bob, 25, bob@example.com, UK
Charlie, 35, charlie@example.com, Canada

## *Step 3: Transform the Data*

Next, we will perform some transformations on the data. For example, we will:

- Remove any rows with missing values.
- Filter out customers who are under 30 years old.

python

```python
# Remove rows with missing values
data_clean = data.dropna()

# Filter customers who are under 30 years old
data_clean = data_clean[data_clean['Age'] >= 30]

# Display the cleaned and filtered data
print(data_clean.head())
```

## *Step 4: Load the Data into a Database*

Now, we will load the transformed data into a **SQLite** database using **SQLAlchemy**. We will create a table for storing customer data and insert the transformed data into this table.

python

```
from sqlalchemy import create_engine

# Create an SQLite database engine
engine = create_engine('sqlite:///customers.db', echo=True)

# Load the cleaned data into the database
data_clean.to_sql('customers', con=engine, if_exists='replace', index=False)

print("Data successfully loaded into the database.")
```

In this step:

- We create an SQLite database named customers.db using **SQLAlchemy**.
- We load the cleaned data into a table called customers. If the table already exists, it will be replaced (if_exists='replace').

### *Step 5: Automate the ETL Process*

To automate the ETL process, we can schedule the script to run at regular intervals (e.g., daily, weekly) using a task scheduler like **Airflow** or **cron** (on Linux/macOS). We can also add error handling to ensure the pipeline runs smoothly.

For simplicity, let's simulate automating this process by running the script periodically.

python

```
import time

# Simulate running the pipeline every 5 seconds (replace with actual scheduling
logic)
while True:
    # Step 1: Extract
    data = pd.read_csv('customers.csv')

    # Step 2: Transform
    data_clean = data.dropna()
    data_clean = data_clean[data_clean['Age'] >= 30]

    # Step 3: Load
    data_clean.to_sql('customers', con=engine, if_exists='replace', index=False)

    print("ETL process completed successfully.")

    # Wait for 5 seconds before running again
    time.sleep(5)
```

This script will run every 5 seconds and perform the ETL tasks, simulating an automated pipeline.

---

In this chapter, we discussed the process of **automating ETL tasks** using Python. We explored how Python can be used for:

- **Extracting** data from different sources like CSV files and databases.
- **Transforming** data by cleaning, filtering, and processing it.
- **Loading** data into a database or data warehouse for analysis.

Python's rich ecosystem of libraries like **pandas**, **SQLAlchemy**, **Airflow**, and **Prefect** allows us to build and automate robust data pipelines. Automating these processes improves efficiency, reduces human error, and ensures that data is always up-to-date and ready for analysis.

In the example, we built a simple ETL pipeline that extracts customer data from a CSV file, performs data cleaning, and loads it into an SQLite database. This pipeline can be expanded to handle more complex data transformations, integrate with cloud services, and scale to handle larger datasets. As businesses increasingly rely on data-driven insights, automating data engineering processes becomes an essential skill for data professionals.

# Chapter 23: Handling Errors and Optimizing Python Automation Scripts

## Debugging and Error Handling in Automation Scripts

One of the key aspects of building reliable automation scripts is ensuring that errors are properly handled and debugging is efficiently conducted. Errors are inevitable when automating tasks, and addressing them appropriately is crucial to maintaining the stability and functionality of the script.

### 1. Common Types of Errors in Python

In automation scripts, the following types of errors are commonly encountered:

- **Syntax Errors**: These occur when Python cannot understand the structure of the code. For example, missing parentheses or incorrect indentation.
- **Runtime Errors**: These occur during the execution of the script, such as division by zero, file not found, or network connection issues.
- **Logical Errors**: These occur when the script runs without crashing, but produces incorrect results due to flawed logic.

## *2. Debugging Python Scripts*

To debug Python scripts effectively, you can use a combination of the following methods:

- **Print Statements**: The simplest form of debugging is inserting print statements at various points in the code to track the flow and inspect variables.

- **Logging**: Python's logging module provides a more robust way of tracking events, errors, and script progress, especially for long-running automation tasks.

- **IDE Debuggers**: Tools like Visual Studio Code, PyCharm, and others provide integrated debuggers with breakpoints and variable inspection capabilities.

- **PDB (Python Debugger)**: Python's built-in interactive debugger allows you to step through your code, inspect variables, and diagnose issues.

**Example: Using logging for debugging**:

python

```
import logging

# Configure logging
logging.basicConfig(level=logging.DEBUG)

def divide(a, b):
    logging.debug(f"Dividing {a} by {b}")
```

```python
try:
    result = a / b
except ZeroDivisionError as e:
    logging.error(f"Error: {e}")
    return None
return result


# Example usage
result = divide(10, 0)
if result is not None:
    logging.info(f"Result: {result}")
else:
    logging.info("Division failed.")
```

In this example, logging helps track the function execution, and errors like division by zero are captured and logged with a detailed message.

### 3. Error Handling in Python

Good error handling ensures that the automation script can recover from errors and continue running. Python provides several mechanisms for error handling:

- **Try-Except Blocks**: These are used to catch and handle specific exceptions.
- **Finally Block**: This block executes whether an exception is raised or not, allowing for cleanup actions.

- **Raising Custom Errors**: You can create custom error messages and raise exceptions to handle unexpected situations.

**Example of error handling**:

python

```
try:
    value = int(input("Enter a number: "))
except ValueError:
    print("Invalid input. Please enter a valid number.")
else:
    print(f"You entered: {value}")
finally:
    print("Execution finished.")
```

In this example, the try block attempts to convert user input to an integer, while the except block handles the case when the input is not a valid number.

---

## Improving Efficiency and Reducing Bottlenecks

Once error handling is in place, it's time to focus on optimizing your automation scripts for better performance and efficiency. A script's performance can often be improved by reducing bottlenecks, which are parts of the code that cause the script to slow down.

## 1. Profiling Your Code

The first step in optimization is identifying the bottlenecks. You can use Python's cProfile module to profile your script and determine where it spends the most time.

**Example of profiling**:

python

import cProfile

```
def slow_function():
    total = 0
    for i in range(10000000):
        total += i
    return total
```

cProfile.run('slow_function()')

This will give you a breakdown of where time is spent in the function. From here, you can focus on optimizing the identified slow sections of your code.

## 2. Optimizing Loops and Data Structures

- **Using List Comprehensions**: List comprehensions are often more efficient than using a for loop, especially for simple operations.

**Example**:

python

```
# Using a for loop
squares = []
for i in range(1000):
    squares.append(i**2)

# Using list comprehension
squares = [i**2 for i in range(1000)]
```

The list comprehension approach is faster and more Pythonic.

- **Optimizing Data Structures**: Choose the right data structure for your needs. For example, if you need fast membership tests, use a set instead of a list.

### 3. Efficient File Handling

I/O operations like reading from and writing to files can be a bottleneck in automation scripts. Optimizing file handling involves:

- Using buffered reading/writing.
- Minimizing the number of times files are opened and closed.
- Using memory-mapped files for large datasets.

---

# Example: Optimizing an Automation Script for Faster Performance

Let's consider an example where we need to automate a task that involves reading a large file, processing data, and writing results to a new file. The naive implementation might read and write the file line by line, which can be slow for large files.

### Step 1: Naive Approach (Slow Performance)

python

```python
def process_file_slow(input_file, output_file):
    with open(input_file, 'r') as infile, open(output_file, 'w') as outfile:
        for line in infile:
            # Simulate data processing
            processed_line = line.strip().upper()
            outfile.write(processed_line + '\n')

# Call the function
process_file_slow('large_input.txt', 'output.txt')
```

This approach reads and writes the file line by line. While simple, this method can be inefficient for large files because it opens and writes to the file repeatedly.

### Step 2: Optimized Approach (Faster Performance)

We can optimize the script by processing the file in chunks and reducing the number of I/O operations.

python

```python
def process_file_optimized(input_file, output_file):
    # Read the entire file at once (assuming it fits in memory)
```

```
with open(input_file, 'r') as infile:
    data = infile.readlines()

# Process the data in memory
processed_data = [line.strip().upper() for line in data]

# Write the processed data in one go
with open(output_file, 'w') as outfile:
    outfile.writelines([line + '\n' for line in processed_data])

# Call the optimized function
process_file_optimized('large_input.txt', 'output.txt')
```

In this optimized approach:

- We read the entire file into memory at once using readlines().
- We process the data in memory, which is faster than writing each line immediately.
- We write the processed data to the file in one go, reducing I/O operations.

This method is much faster than the naive approach, especially for large files.

***Step 3: Further Optimization with Multithreading (If Applicable)***

If the task involves CPU-bound operations or large datasets, consider using **multithreading** or **multiprocessing** to parallelize the work.

**Example with concurrent.futures:**

python

```python
from concurrent.futures import ThreadPoolExecutor

def process_chunk(chunk):
    # Simulate processing a chunk of data
    return [line.strip().upper() for line in chunk]

def process_file_parallel(input_file, output_file, chunk_size=1000):
    with open(input_file, 'r') as infile:
        data = infile.readlines()

    # Split data into chunks
    chunks = [data[i:i + chunk_size] for i in range(0, len(data), chunk_size)]

    # Process the chunks in parallel
    with ThreadPoolExecutor() as executor:
        processed_chunks = list(executor.map(process_chunk, chunks))

    # Write the processed data to the file
    with open(output_file, 'w') as outfile:
        for chunk in processed_chunks:
            outfile.writelines([line + '\n' for line in chunk])

# Call the function
process_file_parallel('large_input.txt', 'output.txt')
```

By using ThreadPoolExecutor, the file is processed in parallel, improving performance for large files or CPU-intensive tasks.

In this chapter, we explored how to **handle errors** and **optimize automation scripts** for better performance in Python. We covered:

- **Debugging and error handling** techniques using try-except blocks, logging, and Python's built-in debugging tools.
- **Optimization strategies**, including using efficient data structures, list comprehensions, minimizing I/O operations, and parallelizing tasks.
- **Real-world example** of optimizing an automation script for processing large files by reducing I/O operations and using multithreading for parallel processing.

By applying these techniques, you can make your Python automation scripts more robust, faster, and capable of handling larger datasets efficiently, ultimately enhancing the automation process.

# Chapter 24: Securing Python-Based Automation Systems

## Best Practices for Securing Automation Workflows

Security is a critical concern when building automation systems, especially when dealing with sensitive data, external APIs, and large-scale workflows. Python-based automation systems often interact with databases, cloud platforms, third-party APIs, and other services, which can expose them to various risks, such as unauthorized access, data breaches, and malicious attacks.

In this chapter, we will discuss best practices for securing your automation workflows. We will cover techniques for securing your code, handling sensitive data, and ensuring the integrity and confidentiality of your automation scripts.

### 1. Secure Your Code and Infrastructure

- **Use Version Control**: Always use a version control system (e.g., Git) to track changes in your codebase. This helps you roll back to previous versions in case of security issues and ensures that only authorized personnel can make changes to the code.

- **Limit Code Access**: Restrict access to your automation scripts and workflows. Ensure that only authorized users or systems can access critical automation scripts.

- **Use Virtual Environments**: Create isolated environments for your automation projects using **virtual environments**. This isolates your project dependencies, preventing conflicts with other systems or applications. This also helps reduce the risk of introducing security vulnerabilities from untrusted packages.

bash

```
python -m venv myenv
source myenv/bin/activate  # On Linux/macOS
myenv\Scripts\activate  # On Windows
```

- **Keep Software Up-to-Date**: Ensure that Python, libraries, and any third-party dependencies are up-to-date. Security vulnerabilities are often patched in newer versions of packages and libraries. Use tools like **pip** or **pipenv** to manage dependencies and regularly check for updates.

bash

```
pip install --upgrade package-name
```

# Handling Sensitive Data, Authentication, and API Security

When automating workflows, particularly with external APIs or third-party services, it's essential to handle sensitive data, such as API keys, passwords, and personal information, securely.

## 1. Managing API Keys and Secrets

- **Never Hardcode Secrets**: Avoid hardcoding sensitive information like API keys or database credentials directly in your code. Instead, use environment variables, configuration files, or secret management tools to store this data securely.

  Example using **environment variables**:

  bash

  ```
  export API_KEY="your-api-key-here"
  ```
  In Python, retrieve the API key securely using the os module:

  python

  ```
  import os
  api_key = os.getenv('API_KEY')
  ```

- **Use Secret Management Services**: For larger applications, consider using cloud-based secret management services like **AWS Secrets Manager**, **Azure Key Vault**, or **HashiCorp Vault**. These tools store and manage sensitive data securely and make it easier to integrate secrets into your automation workflows.

## *2. Authentication and Authorization*

Ensuring proper authentication and authorization is crucial when automating tasks that interact with external services, APIs, or databases.

- **Use Strong Authentication Methods**: Always use strong authentication mechanisms like **OAuth 2.0**, **API keys**, or **JWT (JSON Web Tokens)** for API interactions. Avoid using basic authentication (username/password) unless absolutely necessary.

- **Use Least Privilege Principle**: When authenticating and authorizing your automation scripts, ensure that they have the minimum permissions required to perform their tasks. This reduces the impact of potential security breaches by limiting the actions an attacker can perform.

---

# Example: Implementing OAuth for Secure API Access in Automation Scripts

In many automation workflows, you will need to interact with third-party APIs (e.g., Google APIs, Twitter, etc.). OAuth is a widely used authentication protocol that allows applications to access user data without sharing passwords.

### *Step 1: Setting Up OAuth 2.0 Credentials*

Before implementing OAuth, you need to set up OAuth 2.0 credentials with the service you wish to access. For this example, let's assume you want to access Google APIs.

1. Go to the **Google Developers Console**.
2. Create a new project.
3. Enable the desired API (e.g., Gmail API).
4. Create OAuth 2.0 credentials (Client ID and Client Secret) for your application.
5. Download the **credentials.json** file that contains your OAuth credentials.

### Step 2: Install Necessary Libraries

We will use the **Google OAuth2.0** client library for Python to implement OAuth in our automation script. Install the required libraries:

bash

```
pip install google-auth google-auth-oauthlib google-auth-httplib2 google-api-python-client
```

### Step 3: Implement OAuth 2.0 Authentication in Python

The following Python script demonstrates how to implement OAuth 2.0 authentication to access Google APIs. This example uses the **Google Calendar API** to list upcoming events. It ensures secure access by obtaining OAuth tokens.

python

```python
import os
import pickle
import google.auth
from google_auth_oauthlib.flow import InstalledAppFlow
from googleapiclient.discovery import build

# The scope defines the level of access to the API
SCOPES = ['https://www.googleapis.com/auth/calendar.readonly']

# Step 1: Authenticate the user and obtain OAuth tokens
def authenticate():
    creds = None
    # The token.pickle file stores the user's access and refresh tokens
    # It is created automatically when the authorization flow completes for the first time.
    if os.path.exists('token.pickle'):
        with open('token.pickle', 'rb') as token:
            creds = pickle.load(token)

    # If there are no (valid) credentials available, let the user log in.
    if not creds or not creds.valid:
        if creds and creds.expired and creds.refresh_token:
            creds.refresh(Request())
        else:
            flow = InstalledAppFlow.from_client_secrets_file(
                'credentials.json', SCOPES)
            creds = flow.run_local_server(port=0)
```

```python
        # Save the credentials for the next run
        with open('token.pickle', 'wb') as token:
            pickle.dump(creds, token)

    return creds


# Step 2: Use the credentials to access Google Calendar API
def list_events():
    creds = authenticate()

    try:
        # Build the Google Calendar service
        service = build('calendar', 'v3', credentials=creds)

        # Call the Calendar API to fetch events
        events_result = service.events().list(calendarId='primary', timeMin='2022-
10-01T00:00:00Z',
                                        maxResults=10, singleEvents=True,
                                        orderBy='startTime').execute()
        events = events_result.get('items', [])

        if not events:
            print('No upcoming events found.')
        for event in events:
            start = event['start'].get('dateTime', event['start'].get('date'))
            print(f'{start} - {event["summary"]}')
    except Exception as error:
        print(f'An error occurred: {error}')


if __name__ == '__main__':
```

list_events()

## *Explanation of the Code:*

1.  **OAuth Flow**: The authenticate() function handles the OAuth flow. It first checks if there are existing credentials stored in token.pickle. If the credentials are invalid or expired, the script will prompt the user to authenticate and save the new credentials for future use.

2.  **Accessing Google Calendar**: The list_events() function uses the credentials to build a service object for the Google Calendar API. It retrieves and lists the user's upcoming events.

3.  **Security**: The script ensures that sensitive information like the client ID, client secret, and tokens are stored securely. By using OAuth 2.0, the script never exposes the user's password or requires manual entry each time the automation runs.

---

In this chapter, we covered the importance of securing Python-based automation systems. We discussed:

- **Best practices** for securing code, handling sensitive data, and ensuring the proper authentication and authorization in automation workflows.
- **Error handling** and how to use tools like logging and debugging to identify and resolve issues.
- How to securely access APIs with **OAuth 2.0** in Python, using a practical example that demonstrates how to interact with the Google Calendar API.

By implementing these security practices, you can ensure that your Python automation scripts are robust, secure, and capable of handling sensitive data and interactions with third-party services safely. Security should be an ongoing concern throughout the development of automation systems to protect data, prevent unauthorized access, and maintain the integrity of the systems.

# Chapter 25: Monitoring and Maintaining Automated Systems

## Tools and Techniques for Monitoring Automated Systems

Once you've set up your automation workflows, it's crucial to monitor their performance and ensure they are running smoothly. Monitoring involves tracking the health, performance, and status of automated systems to detect issues before they escalate. This is especially important for long-running processes or systems that handle critical tasks such as backups, data processing, or transaction handling.

### 1. Key Aspects of Monitoring Automated Systems

- **Availability**: Ensure that automated tasks run as scheduled, without failures.

- **Performance**: Monitor resource usage (CPU, memory, disk I/O) to identify any bottlenecks.

- **Error Handling**: Detect and respond to errors or failures, such as API downtime or connection issues.

- **Log Analysis**: Analyze logs for trends, errors, or abnormal activity that could indicate problems.

## 2. Tools for Monitoring

- **Nagios**: An open-source monitoring system that provides monitoring of servers, networks, and applications.
- **Prometheus**: A powerful monitoring and alerting toolkit for containerized applications and microservices.
- **Grafana**: Often used alongside Prometheus, Grafana provides dashboards to visualize metrics and trends.
- **Datadog**: A commercial monitoring service that provides application performance monitoring (APM), log management, and infrastructure monitoring.
- **Zabbix**: An open-source monitoring solution that offers network, server, application, and cloud monitoring.
- **Cloud-native tools**: If you're using cloud platforms, they usually provide native monitoring tools, like **AWS CloudWatch**, **Google Cloud Operations Suite**, and **Azure Monitor**.

## 3. Monitoring with Python

For simple monitoring, Python can be used to create scripts that check the health of your automation tasks. These scripts can poll services, check the status of running tasks, and send notifications when an issue is detected.

## Logging and Alerting for Task Failures

One of the most effective ways to monitor automation systems is through **logging** and **alerting**. Proper logging helps track the progress of automated tasks and assists in debugging when things go wrong. Alerting, on the other hand, immediately notifies system administrators or users when a failure occurs.

### *1. Setting Up Logging in Python*

Python's built-in logging module makes it easy to track events in your automation scripts. Logs can provide critical information about the operation of a script, including error messages, performance metrics, and task status.

Here's how to set up basic logging for automation scripts:

python

```
import logging

# Configure logging
logging.basicConfig(filename='automation.log',          level=logging.INFO,
format='%(asctime)s - %(levelname)s - %(message)s')

def task_function():
    logging.info("Task started.")
    try:
        # Simulate task execution
        result = 10 / 2  # Successful operation
```

```
    logging.info(f"Task result: {result}")
except Exception as e:
    logging.error(f"Task failed: {e}")
finally:
    logging.info("Task completed.")
```

```
# Run the function
task_function()
```

In this example:

- **INFO level logs** track the progress of the task.
- **ERROR level logs** are used to capture failures or exceptions.
- Logs are written to a file (automation.log), which can be reviewed for troubleshooting.

## 2. Setting Up Alerts

Alerting can be integrated with logs to notify users or system administrators about failures or significant events. This can be done using services like **Email**, **Slack**, **SMS**, or **Webhook** notifications.

For example, you can integrate **Email Alerts** using Python's smtplib module to send an email when a task fails.

python

```
import smtplib
from email.mime.text import MIMEText
from email.mime.multipart import MIMEMultipart
```

```python
def send_alert_email(subject, body):
    sender_email = "your_email@example.com"
    receiver_email = "admin@example.com"
    password = "your_email_password"

    msg = MIMEMultipart()
    msg['From'] = sender_email
    msg['To'] = receiver_email
    msg['Subject'] = subject

    msg.attach(MIMEText(body, 'plain'))

    try:
        server = smtplib.SMTP('smtp.example.com', 587)
        server.starttls()
        server.login(sender_email, password)
        text = msg.as_string()
        server.sendmail(sender_email, receiver_email, text)
        server.quit()
        print("Alert email sent successfully!")
    except Exception as e:
        print(f"Failed to send email: {e}")


def task_with_alert():
    try:
        # Simulate a failure
        result = 10 / 0
    except Exception as e:
        send_alert_email("Task Failure Alert", f"The task failed with error: {str(e)}")
```

```
# Trigger the task
task_with_alert()
```

This script:

- Sends an email when an error occurs.
- Uses SMTP to send the email with details of the failure.

### 3. Integrating Alerting with Monitoring Tools

When using monitoring tools like **Prometheus** or **Datadog**, you can set up alerting rules that trigger when specific thresholds or conditions are met. For instance:

- **CPU usage over 80% for 5 minutes**.
- **A task failure or downtime** detected through logs.

Prometheus, for example, can send notifications via **Slack**, **Email**, or other services when a metric exceeds a defined threshold.

---

## Example: Setting Up Monitoring for Automated Backups

Let's look at an example of monitoring an automated backup process. Backups are critical in data protection, and ensuring they complete successfully is important for business continuity.

### Step 1: Script the Backup Process

First, we'll write a Python script that performs a backup and logs the results.

python

```python
import shutil
import logging
import os

# Set up logging
logging.basicConfig(filename='backup.log',                level=logging.INFO,
format='%(asctime)s - %(levelname)s - %(message)s')

def backup_files(source_dir, backup_dir):
    logging.info("Backup process started.")
    try:
        if not os.path.exists(backup_dir):
            os.makedirs(backup_dir)
        shutil.tree(source_dir, backup_dir)
        logging.info(f"Backup successful from {source_dir} to {backup_dir}.")
    except Exception as e:
        logging.error(f"Backup failed: {e}")
        raise
    finally:
        logging.info("Backup process completed.")

# Example usage
backup_files('/path/to/source', '/path/to/backup')
```

## This script:

- Copies all files from the source directory to the backup directory using shutil.tree().
- Logs success or failure with detailed messages.

### *Step 2: Set Up Monitoring for Backup Failures*

We can set up monitoring to detect if the backup script fails or is delayed. You can use a **cron job** (Linux/macOS) or **Task Scheduler** (Windows) to run the backup script periodically, and a **log monitoring tool** like **Logwatch** or **Splunk** to trigger alerts on specific conditions (e.g., "Backup failed" in the logs).

Alternatively, you can integrate monitoring within your Python script, as demonstrated earlier, with **email alerts** or notifications if the backup fails.

For example, you can integrate a script that checks whether the backup was successful by looking for specific log entries:

python

```
def check_backup_log():
    try:
        with open('backup.log', 'r') as log_file:
            logs = log_file.readlines()
        if "Backup failed" in logs[-1]:
            send_alert_email("Backup Failure", "The automated backup process has
failed. Please check the logs.")
        else:
            print("Backup was successful.")
```

```
    except Exception as e:
        print(f"Error reading log: {e}")


# Check the backup log
check_backup_log()
```

### *Step 3: Set Up Cloud Monitoring for Backup Systems*

If your backup system involves cloud services (like **AWS S3**, **Google Cloud Storage**, or **Azure Blob Storage**), you can integrate monitoring tools such as **AWS CloudWatch, Google Cloud Monitoring**, or **Azure Monitor** to keep track of backup status, usage, and any errors. These services can trigger alerts and notifications when failures are detected, enabling real-time monitoring of backup processes.

In this chapter, we discussed the importance of **monitoring and maintaining automated systems**. We covered:

- The **tools and techniques** for monitoring automation workflows, including logging, alerting, and using third-party monitoring solutions.
- The significance of **error handling and logging** to track the health and performance of automated processes.

- A practical example of **setting up monitoring for automated backups**, ensuring that backup tasks are properly logged, and notifying administrators of failures.

By implementing proper monitoring and alerting systems, you can ensure the reliability and efficiency of your automation workflows, quickly detect issues, and maintain operational continuity. This approach is essential for ensuring that critical processes, like backups, run smoothly without manual intervention.

# Chapter 26: Future Trends in AI and Automation with Python

## Exploring Future Technologies and Advancements

The world of **AI** and **automation** is evolving at an unprecedented pace. As new technologies emerge, Python continues to play a significant role in making automation smarter, more efficient, and more accessible across various industries. Let's explore some of the future technologies and advancements that will shape the landscape of AI and automation, and how Python will be at the forefront of these changes.

### 1. Advancements in Machine Learning (ML) and Deep Learning (DL)

The core of many AI and automation systems today is **machine learning** and **deep learning**. In the future, we expect several advancements in these areas, such as:

- **AutoML (Automated Machine Learning)**: Tools like **Google AutoML** and **H2O.ai** are already enabling non-experts to build high-performance machine learning models. This trend will continue, reducing the barriers to AI adoption and allowing even small businesses to benefit from AI-driven automation.

- **Neural Architecture Search (NAS)**: This involves automating the design of neural network architectures using algorithms to improve performance. Python libraries like **Keras Tuner** are already laying the groundwork for this, and future advancements will make it easier to create highly optimized AI models for various tasks.

- **Reinforcement Learning**: RL is already being used in robotics, gaming, and financial sectors. In the future, RL will power more intelligent systems that can autonomously learn to optimize processes without human intervention. Python libraries like **TensorFlow**, **PyTorch**, and **OpenAI Gym** will continue to evolve to support these advances.

## 2. Quantum Computing and AI

Quantum computing is one of the most exciting and disruptive technologies on the horizon. While it's still in its early stages, it promises to revolutionize how we approach complex problems, including those in AI and automation.

- **Quantum AI**: Quantum computers can potentially solve problems that classical computers cannot, particularly in optimization and large-scale data analysis. For example, quantum machine learning algorithms may speed up tasks like feature selection, training large neural networks, and solving optimization problems in real-time.

- **Python's Role**: As quantum computing develops, Python will continue to be a primary language for working with quantum algorithms. Libraries such as **Qiskit** (IBM), **PennyLane**, and **Cirq** (Google) are already providing the tools to integrate quantum computing with machine learning models, making quantum-enhanced AI more accessible to developers.

### 3. Edge Computing and AI at the Edge

**Edge computing** refers to processing data closer to where it is generated rather than in a centralized cloud. This is particularly useful for real-time processing, low-latency applications, and IoT (Internet of Things) devices.

- **AI on the Edge**: As IoT devices become more prevalent, there will be an increasing need for AI models to run directly on these devices. This will enable faster decision-making and reduce the reliance on cloud infrastructure.
- **Python's Role**: Python will remain a key player in edge computing by supporting libraries like **TensorFlow Lite** and **PyTorch Mobile** that allow developers to deploy AI models on mobile devices and edge hardware like Raspberry Pi, Nvidia Jetson, and specialized AI chips. This trend will drive automation in environments where real-time responses are

critical, such as autonomous vehicles, smart cities, and industrial applications.

## The Role of AI and Automation in Different Industries

AI and automation are already transforming various industries. However, in the future, their role will be even more pronounced, revolutionizing how businesses operate and creating new opportunities for innovation.

### 1. Healthcare

AI and automation are poised to reshape the healthcare industry, enhancing patient care, reducing costs, and improving efficiency. Here are some areas where AI will play a crucial role:

- **Personalized Medicine**: AI-powered systems will analyze genetic data, patient histories, and lifestyle information to recommend personalized treatments. Python will continue to be the go-to language for developing models that can process and analyze medical data, with libraries like **TensorFlow**, **Keras**, and **scikit-learn** being widely used for medical applications.

- **Medical Imaging**: AI-driven image recognition algorithms will help doctors detect diseases like cancer, heart conditions, and neurological disorders more accurately. Python libraries like **OpenCV** and **PyTorch** will continue to be key tools for image processing and analysis in medical fields.

- **Robotic Surgery**: Automation will play a huge role in robotic surgery, where robots perform surgeries with high precision. Python will power the AI algorithms that guide these systems, making them smarter, faster, and more capable.

## 2. Manufacturing and Industry 4.0

The rise of **Industry 4.0** refers to the integration of smart technologies in manufacturing, including robotics, AI, IoT, and automation.

- **Smart Factories**: AI and automation will enable real-time monitoring, predictive maintenance, and autonomous production lines. Python's role in managing data from sensors and IoT devices, as well as running machine learning models to predict failures and optimize production schedules, will be critical.
- **Supply Chain Optimization**: AI will help optimize logistics, reduce waste, and improve inventory management. Python libraries such as **pandas**, **NumPy**, and **scikit-learn** will continue to be used to analyze and model supply chain data, automating processes and improving decision-making.

## 3. Finance and Trading

In finance, AI is already being used to detect fraudulent activity, optimize trading strategies, and manage risk. The future will bring even more AI-driven financial automation:

- **Automated Trading**: AI algorithms will autonomously trade based on market conditions, adjusting strategies in real-time. Python, with its rich ecosystem of libraries like **Pandas**, **NumPy**, and **QuantConnect**, will continue to be integral to developing these algorithms.

- **Risk Management**: AI will help financial institutions predict market risks and optimize investment portfolios. Python libraries such as **SciPy** and **statsmodels** will remain essential in developing models to forecast market trends and perform risk assessments.

### 4. Autonomous Vehicles

The development of **autonomous vehicles** is one of the most exciting applications of AI and automation. Python will play a key role in developing the AI systems that power self-driving cars:

- **Computer Vision**: AI models will help autonomous vehicles understand their environment through cameras, LIDAR, and radar. Python's libraries like **OpenCV**, **TensorFlow**, and **PyTorch** will be at the forefront of image processing and object detection in autonomous vehicles.

- **Navigation and Decision-Making**: AI algorithms will make real-time decisions for navigation, obstacle avoidance, and route optimization. Python will continue to be a primary language for developing these systems, working with tools like **ROS** (Robot Operating System) for autonomous vehicle development.

## Example: How Python Will Continue to Shape Automation in the Future

Let's consider the example of **smart city automation** in the future. In smart cities, AI and automation systems will manage everything from traffic flow to energy consumption. Python will play a central role in developing these systems, making use of AI algorithms, IoT devices, and automation workflows.

### *Example Use Case: Smart Traffic Management in a Smart City*

- **Data Collection**: Python-based automation systems will collect data from traffic sensors, cameras, and GPS devices in vehicles. This data will be used to analyze traffic patterns and detect congestion.
- **AI Analysis**: Machine learning models developed in Python will predict traffic conditions, detect accidents, and identify optimal routes in real-time. Python's libraries like **scikit-**

**learn** for machine learning and **Pandas** for data manipulation will be critical for processing and analyzing this data.

- **Automation**: Python scripts will automatically adjust traffic lights, control traffic flow, and even notify drivers about optimal routes, all without human intervention. The Python-based automation system will constantly learn from traffic patterns and improve its performance over time, utilizing reinforcement learning or predictive analytics.

- **Integration with IoT**: The Python-based system will seamlessly integrate with IoT devices, such as smart streetlights and autonomous vehicles, creating a fully automated smart city ecosystem.

This is just one example of how Python will continue to play a significant role in shaping the future of automation, not just in transportation, but across various industries.

In this chapter, we explored the **future trends in AI and automation** and how Python will continue to shape this evolution. From advancements in machine learning and quantum computing to the role of AI in industries like healthcare, finance, and smart cities, Python remains at the forefront of automation technology.

- **AI and machine learning** will continue to drive automation, making systems smarter and more efficient.
- **Edge computing and IoT** will expand the scope of automation, enabling real-time processing at the source of data generation.
- Python will remain an essential tool in building and deploying automation systems, with its extensive libraries, ease of integration, and flexibility.

As we look to the future, Python's role in AI and automation will only grow, helping to automate increasingly complex systems and improve the way we live and work.